ITALIAN COOKING
in Your Instant Pot®

60 Flavorful Homestyle Favorites
Made Faster Than Ever

Tawnie Graham, RDN
Creator of Kroll's Korner

PAGE STREET
PUBLISHING CO.

PAGE STREET
PUBLISHING CO.

Copyright © 2023 Tawnie Graham

First published in 2023 by
Page Street Publishing Co.
27 Congress Street, Suite 1511
Salem, MA 01970
www.pagestreetpublishing.com

Distributed by Macmillan, sales in Canada by The Canadian Manda Group.

27   26   25   24   23   1 2 3 4 5

ISBN-13: 978-1-64567-987-5
ISBN-10: 1-64567-987-X

Library of Congress Control Number: 2022946891

Cover and book design by Molly Kate Young for Page Street Publishing Co.
Cover and Author photography by Ellie Koleen
Food Photography by Tawnie Graham

Printed and bound in the United States of America

To my daughter, Arya Rose.

Find what you love to do and pursue that precise thing with all your heart.

I love you to the moon and back infinity times.

TABLE OF CONTENTS

STARTERS AND SIDES   107

STAPLE SAUCES   133

INTRODUCTION

Hi! My name is Tawnie. You may know me as the creator behind the food blog Kroll's Korner. I am a registered dietitian, wife and mom, and I like to make cooking fun and approachable.

I am thrilled you have this book in your hands! It's been a dream of mine for years to write a book and what better time to write a book than with a toddler running around? All the recipes you will find in this book are easy to follow, easy to make and most important, packed with flavor. I can't wait for you to enjoy what this book has to offer.

With this Instant Pot® Italian cookbook, home cooks can now enjoy flavor-packed, Italian-inspired recipes with minimal effort and in most cases, these recipes take less than an hour from start to finish. Inside this book, you will find something for everyone. There are plenty of uber-delicious pastas to choose from, an entire chapter on satisfying soups, options for those who do not eat meat and of course a variety of meaty options. All my recipes are made using fresh, high-quality ingredients that come together effortlessly creating blow-your-mind delicious family meals.

If you're anything like me, you don't have time for lengthy ingredient lists, complicated recipes, or long cook times. With these Instant Pot recipes, I am confident you'll be able to get a delicious meal on the table quickly. You'll find Italian classics like Linguine alla Carbonara (page 33), Easy Pasta e Fagioli (page 94) and my own recipe spins like Creamy Tomato White Bean Soup with Pesto (page 89).

In this book, I will show you that cooking with an Instant Pot is safe, straightforward and most important, super tasty! I know you'll love your Instant Pot even more after making just one of the recipes in this book!

These recipes are Italian American and I am using inspiration from my own family's cooking. My philosophy is to make realistic and approachable meals for busy people (which I think includes all of us, right?). Get ready for delicious recipes with Italian flare that anyone can make.

Let's have some fun cooking amazing recipes in the Instant Pot, and don't forget to grab a glass or two of wine!

Tawnie Graham

NOTES: All these recipes were tested in the Instant Pot® Duo™ Plus 6-quart Multi-Use Pressure Cooker.

The Instant Pot has a "less/normal/more" function for the sauté feature. Pressing the sauté button multiple times will switch between these modes. Unless directed, most recipes sauté in the normal mode.

Praiseworthy Pastas

A creamy, luscious sauce with a heavy dusting of freshly grated Parmesan is my love language. As far back as I can remember, pasta has been a staple in my life. Growing up as a long-distance runner meant a lot of pasta nights in our home. Now, as a busy working mom, the Instant Pot has brought a touch of magic into our kitchen because it speeds up the cooking time of our all-time favorite pasta dishes.

Whether you are craving straight up comfort food or yearning for an easy but nutritious pasta, you'll be able to find something you love in this chapter. My Date Night Tuscan Chicken Pasta (page 11) only takes 30 minutes to make , and you can never go wrong with pasta blanketed in a creamy, tomato-kissed sauce. If you're looking for a pasta with enough pizzazz to impress your loved ones or friends but don't have a ton of time on your hands, my Cheesy Beef Lasagna (page 15) and my Speedy "Baked" Ziti (page 12) will help you make dinner stress free. Plus, you'll be happy to have leftovers for lunch the following day!

Making pasta in the Instant Pot is arguably easier, faster and tastier than any stovetop version and the hands-off time is one of the most attractive parts about these dishes. No more standing over the stove, waiting for water to boil and constantly stirring. The magic all happens in the pressure cooker to create beautiful, big-on-flavor pastas.

I can't wait for you to dive headfirst into these easy-to-make, yet impressive and indulgent pastas (pssst—don't forget the shower of grated Parmesan on your pasta before you take a swim)!

DATE NIGHT TUSCAN CHICKEN PASTA

1½ lb (681 g) boneless, skinless chicken breasts

2 tsp (3 g) Italian seasoning

2 tsp (12 g) kosher salt

1 tsp paprika

1 tsp red pepper chili flakes

¼ tsp black pepper

2 tbsp (30 ml) olive oil

2 tbsp (28 g) unsalted butter

1 shallot, minced

1 small red bell pepper, seeded and diced small

4 cloves garlic, minced

5.3 oz (150 g) oil-packed sun-dried tomatoes, oil drained

4 cups (960 ml) chicken broth

12 oz (341 g) farfalle pasta, uncooked

1 cup (100 g) freshly grated Parmesan cheese

4 oz (116 g) cream cheese, softened

4¾ cups (143 g) baby spinach, roughly chopped

Garnish

Parmesan cheese

Torn basil leaves, for serving

This Tuscan Chicken Pasta is a fail-proof, creamy, dreamy weeknight pasta dish. And it's one of those recipes that is just a total mom win, not just because everyone will slurp it up, but because there is minimal chopping and sautéing involved! If you're thinking of making pasta tonight, I can't recommend this dish enough.

1. Cut the chicken into small bite-sized pieces (about 1-inch [2.5-cm] cubes) and place them in a large mixing bowl. Add the Italian seasoning, salt, paprika, chili flakes and pepper. Stir to combine and set aside.

2. Add the olive oil and butter to the Instant Pot. Press "Sauté" and wait a minute or two for the butter to melt. Add in the shallot and red bell pepper and sauté until softened, for 2 to 3 minutes. Add in the garlic and stir for 30 seconds.

3. Add in the seasoned chicken and cook for 4 to 5 minutes, or until the chicken is lightly browned on the outside. It won't be cooked completely though and that's OK. Add in the sun-dried tomatoes and chicken broth and stir. Pour in the pasta and gently submerge the pasta into the broth, but DO NOT STIR.

4. Press "Cancel" to exit the sauté mode. Secure the lid. Press the "Pressure Cook" button until the display light is under "HIGH" and use the "-/+" button to adjust the time to 5 minutes. Be sure the valve on top is set to sealing.

5. When the pasta is done, quick release the steam. Once the pin drops, remove the lid. Add in the Parmesan cheese and cream cheese. Stir until combined. Lastly, stir in the spinach and allow it to wilt for one minute. Garnish with Parmesan and basil, if desired, and enjoy!

TAWNIE'S TIP: You'll notice a lot of Instant Pot instructions mention "DO NOT STIR." This is particularly important for pasta recipes and dishes with red sauce. For pasta recipes, not stirring prevents the pasta from sticking to the bottom of the pot. And for tomato-based recipes, it's important to not stir to avoid the dreaded "BURN" message. Since the heating element is at the bottom of the pot, the sugars have a higher chance of caramelizing and setting off the "BURN" message.

SPEEDY "BAKED" ZITI

YIELD: 8 SERVINGS
TOTAL TIME: 30 MINUTES

1½ tbsp (20 ml) olive oil

1 lb (454 g) ground hot Italian sausage

1 medium yellow onion, diced

3 cloves garlic, pressed

2 tsp (6 g) Italian seasoning

1 tsp kosher salt

Black pepper, freshly ground to taste

½ tsp red pepper chili flakes

2 tbsp (32 g) tomato paste

2 cups (480 ml) beef broth

1 lb (454 g) ziti noodles, uncooked

24 oz (680 g) jarred or homemade marinara sauce

1 cup (246 g) whole milk ricotta cheese

1 cup (112 g) fresh mozzarella cheese, grated

¾ cup (75 g) finely grated Parmesan cheese

2 tbsp (8 g) fresh flat leaf Italian parsley

Garnish

Parmesan cheese
Fresh basil

This speedy ziti is a major family favorite recipe! It's comforting and easy to prepare and is such a satisfying meal. It packs in tons of flavor thanks to the spicy ground Italian sausage, marinara and all the cheesy goodness. This recipe comes together in just 30 minutes, which is much faster than the traditional ziti. I already know you're going to be obsessed with this one. Pair with a side salad and you're all set!

1. Choose the "Sauté" normal mode on the Instant Pot and add the olive oil. Add the sausage and onion and cook, breaking up the meat with a wooden spoon until the onion is fragrant and the meat is no longer pink, approximately 5 minutes. Add the garlic and stir for approximately 30 seconds. Season with Italian seasoning, salt, pepper and chili flakes. Stir to combine. Add the tomato paste and stir.

2. Pour in the beef broth and then add the uncooked ziti noodles. Add the marinara on top and DO NOT STIR. Press "Cancel" to exit the sauté mode.

3. Secure the lid. Press the "Pressure Cook" button until the display light is under "HIGH" and use the "-/+" button to adjust the time to 6 minutes. Be sure the valve on top is set to sealing. Once the ziti is done, quick release the steam. Once the pin drops, remove the lid.

4. In a medium-sized bowl, combine the ricotta cheese, mozzarella cheese, Parmesan cheese and the parsley.

5. Dollop the cheese on top of the pasta. Replace the lid back on the Instant Pot so the cheese melts over the pasta. Serve with additional Parmesan cheese or freshly torn basil on top and enjoy!

TAWNIE'S TIP: This recipe makes quite a bit of pasta. Any of your leftovers can be stored in an airtight container in the refrigerator for up to 4 days.

CHEESY BEEF LASAGNA

For the ground beef

1 tbsp (15 ml) olive oil

1 lb (454 g) ground beef

1 medium white onion, finely diced

2 tsp (12 g) salt

1 tsp onion powder

1 tsp garlic powder

1 tsp Italian seasoning

½ tsp red pepper chili flakes

⅛ tsp black pepper

For the ricotta

2 cups (492 g) whole milk ricotta

1 cup (30 g) baby spinach, finely chopped

½ cup (50 g) freshly grated Parmesan cheese

1 large egg

1 tbsp (4 g) fresh flat leaf Italian parsley, minced

1 tbsp (2 g) fresh basil, minced

Growing up, every year on Christmas Eve, my mom made a home-made lasagna for the family. After I made this recipe my mom told me, "I think this needs to be the new Christmas Eve lasagna!" I'd happily take over the reins because making lasagna in the Instant Pot is now my go-to method! It's filled with layers of meat and cheese (duh!) and there is just something so cute about lasagna in a circle, don't you think?! Finish off the lasagna under the broiler in the oven for piping hot, golden bubbly cheese.

1. Add the olive oil to the Instant Pot. Press "Sauté" and wait 1 to 2 minutes for the olive oil to get hot. Add in the ground beef and cook, breaking it up with a wooden spoon for approximately 3 to 4 minutes. When the meat is about halfway cooked, add in the onion and cook until the meat is no longer pink and onion is soft and fragrant, about 3 to 4 minutes longer. Add in all the seasonings and stir to combine. Press "Cancel" to exit the sauté mode. Transfer the meat and onion to a bowl and set aside. Clean out the inner pot and replace it in the Instant Pot.

2. In a medium-sized mixing bowl, combine the whole milk ricotta, baby spinach, Parmesan cheese, egg, parsley and basil for the ricotta mixture. Set aside.

3. Prepare a 7 x 3–inch (18 x 8–cm) springform pan. (Or you can use the Fat Daddio's® 7 x 3–inch (18 x 8–cm) cheesecake pan with a removable bottom.) Wrap the bottom of the pan in a double layer of foil. Then, create a foil sling by taking a long strip of foil and folding it lengthwise into thirds, like a letter. Bend the ends up so they make "handles." Place the sling under the springform pan to make it easier to lift the lasagna in and out of the pot.

(continued)

For the lasagna

24 oz (680 g) jarred marinara sauce

8 sheets (137 g) uncooked, oven-ready lasagna sheets

1 cup (112 g) low moisture mozzarella, freshly shredded

¼ cup (25 g) freshly shredded Parmesan cheese

4. Build the lasagna. Pour a thin layer of marinara sauce down on the bottom of the springform or pop pan. Break 2 of the lasagna sheets into pieces and place them down on the sauce, like puzzle pieces. Add a layer of sauce on top of the noodles, then some of the ground beef, then a layer of the ricotta (about ⅔ cup (180 g) each of meat and ricotta). Repeat this layering process two more times (noodles, sauce, beef and then the ricotta). Finally, end with one last layer of the broken noodles and the last of the marinara sauce. Top with the mozzarella and the Parmesan cheese. The lasagna will be full to the top. Cover with foil (spray it with non-stick spray so it doesn't stick to the cheese).

5. Pour 1½ cups (360 ml) water into the Instant Pot and then place the lasagna onto the trivet in the Instant Pot. Secure the lid. Press the "Pressure Cook" button until the display light is under "HIGH" and use the "-/+" button to adjust the time to 25 minutes. Be sure the valve on top is set to sealing. Once the lasagna is done, allow the pressure to naturally release for 10 minutes. Quick release any of the remaining pressure and once the pin drops, remove the lid.

6. Using potholders, grab hold of the foil sling handles to carefully lift the lasagna up. Place on a foil-lined baking sheet. Remove the top piece of foil and broil in the oven for 2 minutes or until the cheese is golden and bubbly. Remove the lasagna from the oven and allow it to rest for at least 15 minutes. Run a butter knife around the edges of the lasagna before removing from the springform pan. Slice and enjoy warm!

TAWNIE'S TIP: If using a 7 x 3-inch (18 x 8-cm) cake pan with a removable bottom, place the cooked lasagna on top of a large mason jar or a large glass to lift the lasagna out of the pan. Then carefully transfer to a cutting board to cut into slices and serve.

TOMATO BASIL SAUSAGE RISOTTO

YIELD: 8 SERVINGS
TOTAL TIME: 45 MINUTES

4 cups (960 ml) chicken broth, plus more if needed

2 tbsp (30 ml) olive oil, divided

1 lb (454 g) sweet Italian sausage

½ large yellow onion, finely chopped

3 cloves garlic, minced

2 cups (394 g) Arborio rice, uncooked

½ cup (120 ml) pinot grigio, sauvignon blanc or a dry chardonnay

½ cup (120 g) passata (tomato puree)

1 cup (140 g) cherry tomatoes, halved

1 tsp kosher salt

If you've ever made risotto on the stovetop, you know it's a bit of an arm workout. Usually, I don't mind since I have a glass of wine in the other hand, but since the Instant Pot takes all the arm work out of making risotto, now I can have a glass of wine in each hand! Just kidding, wink wink. This Tomato Basil Sausage Risotto delivers an ultra-creamy, luscious meal jam-packed with juicy tomatoes, fragrant basil and hearty sausage. It's relatively hands-off considering the traditional method and a perfect all-in-one meal for the busiest nights.

1. Heat the chicken broth in a medium saucepan over medium heat. Keep it on low simply to keep the broth warm.

2. Add 1 tablespoon (15 ml) of olive oil to the Instant Pot. Press "Sauté" and wait 1 to 2 minutes for the oil to get hot. Add in the sweet Italian sausage and cook, breaking it up with a wooden spoon for 5 minutes or until no longer pink. Remove the sausage to a bowl and set aside.

3. Add the remaining olive oil in the pot and add in the onion. Cook for 2 to 3 minutes or until the onion is fragrant. Add in the garlic and stir for 30 seconds. Add in the Arborio rice and stir to toast the rice for 2 minutes.

4. Deglaze the bottom of the pan with the white wine. Let the wine cook for another 2 to 3 minutes. Add in the warm broth, passata, cherry tomatoes and salt. Stir to combine and bring to a gentle simmer. Then press the "Cancel" button to turn the sauté function off.

(continued)

¾ cup (18 g) loosely packed fresh basil, chopped, plus more for garnish

¾ cup (75 g) finely grated Parmesan cheese, plus more for garnish

3 tbsp (42 g) unsalted butter

5. Secure the lid and press the "Pressure Cook" button until the display light is under "HIGH" and use the "-/+" button to adjust the time to 6 minutes. Be sure the valve on top is set to sealing. Once the risotto is done, allow the pressure to naturally release for 5 minutes. Quick release any of the remaining pressure and once the pin drops, remove the lid. Give the risotto a good stir. Add the cooked sausage back in and stir to combine.

6. Add in the basil, Parmesan cheese and butter. Stir to combine. Season to taste with salt and pepper. Garnish with additional basil and Parmesan cheese and serve warm.

TAWNIE'S TIPS:

- The perfect risotto consistency should be able to slightly spread when on a plate but stay firmly together when the plate is wiggled back and forth. If the risotto is too thick for your liking, add a little more broth to thin it out.

- If you'd like to make this vegetarian, you can simply omit the sausage and use vegetable broth instead of chicken broth.

30-MINUTE PENNE ALLA VODKA

YIELD: 6–8 SERVINGS
TOTAL TIME: 30 MINUTES

3 tbsp (42 g) unsalted butter

1 medium yellow onion, diced

2 cloves garlic, thinly sliced

1 tsp kosher salt

½ tsp red pepper chili flakes

1 tbsp (16 g) tomato paste

½ cup (120 ml) vodka

1 lb (454 g) penne pasta, uncooked

2½ cups (600 ml) filtered water

24 oz (680 g) jarred marinara sauce

½ cup (120 ml) heavy cream

2 oz (55 g) Parmigiano-Reggiano, finely grated

Garnish

Cracked black pepper

Fresh basil

Additional Parmigiano-Reggiano

Extra creamy, saucy penne alla vodka is a 30-minute pasta made with minimal effort and simple ingredients. The vodka adds depth, flavor and helps to balance out the sweetness of the tomatoes and heavy cream. Finish off the penne with some cracked black pepper, freshly torn basil leaves and a generous amount of Parmigiano-Reggiano and devour!

1. Press "Sauté" and choose the less mode on the Instant Pot and melt the butter, moving it around the pot to melt evenly. Add the onion and cook, stirring occasionally, until it is fragrant and translucent, for 3 minutes. Add the garlic and stir for 30 seconds. Season with salt and chili flakes.

2. Add the tomato paste and stir to coat the onion. Pour the vodka in and combine, cook for 2 minutes and then press the "Cancel" button to turn the sauté function off.

3. Pour in the penne noodles, followed by the water. Press the noodles down gently, making sure most of the pasta is covered by water.

4. Pour the marinara sauce on top and DO NOT STIR. Secure the lid. Press the "Pressure Cook" button until the display light is under "HIGH" and use the "-/+" button to adjust the time to 4 minutes. Be sure the valve on top is set to sealing. Once the penne is done, quick release the steam. Once the pin drops, remove the lid.

5. Stir the pasta. Add in the heavy cream and Parmigiano-Reggiano and stir again. The sauce will thicken as it cools. Taste and adjust the seasonings as desired and serve with cracked black pepper, freshly torn basil and Parmigiano-Reggiano on top.

TAWNIE'S TIPS:

- While this pasta is delicious on its own, I also love adding chicken or shrimp! Just pan fry 8 ounces (227 g) of chicken or shrimp, season with some salt and pepper and stir into the pasta with the heavy cream and Parmigiano-Reggiano.

- Feel free to add in a couple generous handfuls of fresh baby spinach at the end before serving.

FAST SPAGHETTI BOLOGNESE

YIELD: 6 SERVINGS
TOTAL TIME: 45 MINUTES

2 tbsp (28 g) unsalted butter

1 lb (454 g) ground beef

1 small yellow onion, diced

1 cup (110 g) carrots, grated

3 ribs celery

4 oz (113 g) white mushrooms, grated

1 tsp kosher salt

½ tsp freshly grated black pepper

⅛ tsp freshly grated nutmeg

3 cloves garlic, minced

3 tbsp (48 g) tomato paste

1 tbsp (15 g) granulated sugar

⅓ cup (80 ml) pinot grigio, sauvignon blanc or a dry chardonnay

1¾ cup (420 ml) beef broth

1 (15-oz [425-g]) can crushed tomatoes

12 oz (340 g) spaghetti, uncooked, broken in half

½ cup (120 ml) heavy cream

¼ cup (15 g) fresh flat leaf Italian parsley, chopped

Garnish

Parmesan cheese

Fresh basil

If you have this book in your hands, you know how much of a game changer the Instant Pot is. This recipe specifically has been on repeat in our house at least every other week. My daughter loves it, my husband can't get enough of it and I love making it. It's an all-in-one type of meal, but I also love serving it with a roasted veggie or side salad. This sauce gets lots of body and texture from the meat, vegetables and cream. If you prefer to make the sauce without the spaghetti, check out my Weeknight Bolognese Sauce recipe on page 136.

1. Add the butter to the Instant Pot. Press "Sauté" and wait 1 or 2 minutes for the butter to melt. Add in the ground beef and cook, breaking it up with a wooden spoon for 3 to 4 minutes. When the meat is about halfway cooked, add in the onion, carrots, celery and mushrooms. Season with salt, pepper and nutmeg. Cook, stirring occasionally for another 5 minutes or until the meat is cooked and the veggies are fragrant.

2. Add in the garlic, tomato paste and sugar and stir for 30 seconds to combine. Deglaze the bottom of the Instant Pot with white wine. Cook for 2 minutes. Then, press "Cancel" to exit the sauté mode.

3. Add in the beef broth and crushed tomatoes. Add the uncooked spaghetti on top in a crisscross pattern and gently press down into the beef broth, but DO NOT STIR.

4. Secure the lid and press the "Pressure Cook" button until the display light is under "HIGH" and use the "-/+" button to adjust the time to 9 minutes. Be sure the valve on top is set to sealing. Once the pasta is done, quick release the steam. Once the pin drops, remove the lid. Stir the pasta to combine the noodles with the sauce.

5. Stir in the heavy cream and fresh parsley. Taste and adjust seasonings, as desired. Garnish with Parmesan cheese and fresh basil and enjoy!

TAWNIE'S TIP: I love making this recipe with a mix of meat too! You can find pre-mixed ground meat combinations at most grocery stores now.

CREAMY WHITE PESTO CHICKEN PASTA

YIELD: 4 SERVINGS

TOTAL TIME: 30 MINUTES

8 oz (226 g) cavatappi pasta, uncooked

2 cups (480 ml) chicken broth

1 lb (454 g) boneless, skinless, chicken thighs or breasts, cut into bite-sized pieces (about 1-inch [2.5-cm] cubes)

2 cups (480 ml) whole milk

¼ cup (57 g) unsalted butter

¼ cup (31 g) all-purpose flour

3 cloves garlic, pressed

1 tsp kosher salt

¾ tsp dried oregano

½ tsp red pepper chili flakes

1 cup (100 g) finely shredded Parmesan cheese

1 tbsp (15 ml) fresh lemon juice

½ tsp lemon zest

1 tbsp (16 g) Everyday Pesto (page 144) or use a store-bought pesto

Garnish

Toasted pine nuts

Fresh basil

Whole milk ricotta (if desired)

You know when you make a pasta recipe and you think "Wow, that's outrageously good." That is exactly what you'll be saying when you make this pasta! You'll love how the bite-sized chicken pieces act like a mop for the creamy white pesto sauce and of course how easy it is to make.

1. Add the pasta to the Instant Pot and pour the chicken broth over the pasta. Add the chicken on top of the pasta and broth. DO NOT STIR.

2. Secure the lid. Press the "Pressure Cook" button until the display light is under "HIGH" and use the "-/+" button to adjust the time to 5 minutes. Be sure the valve on top is set to sealing. Once the pasta is done, perform a "controlled quick release," which means press on the stream release valve for about 5 seconds and then stop for a couple seconds. Repeat this until all the pressure has been released. If you don't release the pressure this way, the valve will spit out a lot of water and it can get messy.

3. Press "Cancel" and remove the lid. Drain the pasta and chicken and set aside.

4. Microwave the milk in a glass measuring cup for 30 to 45 seconds, or until slightly warm to the touch.

5. Press "Sauté" and choose the less mode. Add the butter and allow it to melt, moving it around the pot so it melts evenly. Add the flour and whisk to form a paste and continue whisking for 1 minute. Begin to add the milk in a slow, steady stream, whisking constantly.

6. After 3 to 4 minutes, the sauce will thicken and begin to gently bubble. Add the garlic, salt, oregano and chili flakes. Whisk to combine. Then, stir in the Parmesan cheese until it is well combined. Once the sauce is bubbly and can coat the back of a spoon, add in the pasta and chicken. Stir. Add the lemon juice, lemon zest and pesto. Stir again. Serve warm with toasted pine nuts, basil and a dollop of ricotta if desired.

TAWNIE'S TIP: Do you have more than one sealing ring? It's always a good idea to have 2 to 3 on hand and switch them out every 6 to 12 months, because the sealing ring can retain the aromas of previously cooked foods.

ORECCHIETTE WITH BACON AND SUN-DRIED TOMATOES

YIELD: 4 SERVINGS
TOTAL TIME: 30 MINUTES

1 tbsp (15 ml) olive oil

1 tbsp (14 g) unsalted butter

2 slices thick-cut bacon, chopped into small pieces

¼ cup (35 g) shallots, minced

2 cloves garlic, minced

5 cups (335 g) Tuscan kale, stems removed and chopped

½ cup (27 g) sun-dried tomatoes

1 tsp kosher salt

¼ tsp freshly ground black pepper

½ tsp red pepper chili flakes

2¾ cup (660 ml) water

8 oz (227 g) orecchiette pasta, uncooked

½ cup (116 g) mascarpone cheese

½ cup (50 g) freshly grated Parmesan cheese

1 tbsp (15 ml) lemon juice, freshly squeezed

Garnish

Freshly grated Parmesan cheese

Toasted pine nuts (optional)

Orecchiette pasta makes for the perfect little sauce holders for this light and creamy mascarpone sauce. The balance between the savory bacon and flavor-packed sun-dried tomatoes is one of our favorite combinations of flavors. You'll love the orecchiette pasta and the chewy charm of the sun-dried tomatoes against the natural brightness of fresh lemon and Tuscan kale.

1. Add the olive oil and butter to the Instant Pot. Press "Sauté" and wait 1 to 2 minutes for the butter to melt.

2. Add the bacon and cook until it's rendered, 6 to 7 minutes. Then, add in the shallots and cook for about 2 minutes. Stir in the garlic for 30 seconds. Deglaze the bottom of the pot with a splash of water.

3. Add in the kale and cook until the kale wilts, 4 to 5 minutes. Then, add in the sun-dried tomatoes, salt, pepper and chili flakes, and stir. Add in the water, followed by the orecchiette pasta. Gently press the pasta down into liquid, but DO NOT STIR.

4. Press "Cancel" to exit the sauté mode. Secure the lid. Press the "Pressure Cook" button until the display light is under "HIGH" and use the "-/+" button to adjust the time to 5 minutes. Be sure the valve on top is set to sealing. Once the pasta is done, allow the pressure to naturally release for 5 minutes. Quick release any of the remaining pressure and once the pin drops, remove the lid.

5. Stir in the mascarpone cheese and Parmesan cheese until combined. Add the lemon juice and stir. Serve with additional grated Parmesan cheese and toasted pine nuts, if using, and enjoy!

TAWNIE'S TIP: If you don't have mascarpone, you can substitute cream cheese instead!

CHICKEN PARMESAN PASTA

YIELD: 6-8 SERVINGS
TOTAL TIME: 45 MINUTES

For the pasta

2 (1.5-lbs [682-g]) boneless, skinless chicken breasts cut into bite-sized pieces

2 tsp (3 g) Italian seasoning

1 tsp kosher salt

1 tsp garlic powder

1 tsp onion powder

½ tsp black pepper

½ tsp red pepper chili flakes (optional)

1 tbsp (15 ml) olive oil

1 lb (454 g) fusilli pasta, uncooked

24 oz (680 g) jarred marinara sauce

3 cups (720 ml) water

1 cup (112 g) low-moisture mozzarella, shredded

½ cup (50 g) freshly grated Parmesan cheese

For the breadcrumb topping

1 tbsp (15 ml) olive oil

1 cup (56 g) panko breadcrumbs

4 cloves garlic, minced

¼ cup (25 g) shredded Parmesan cheese

¼ cup (15 g) fresh flat leaf Italian parsley, chopped

Garnish

Fresh basil

Flat leaf Italian parsley

Parmesan cheese

This recipe takes all the flavors you love from Chicken Parmesan and bundles it up into an outrageously delicious pasta dish. Trust me when I say to not skip out on the crunchy, golden-brown breadcrumb topping spiked with fresh Parmesan. It's totally worth the extra step of using the stove! Think of it like the breadcrumb coating on a classic Chicken Parmesan. It's the perfect way to complete this pasta in my humble opinion. It's a lip-smacking, downright delicious, easy meal that your family will love!

1. Add the chicken to a medium-sized mixing bowl and stir in the Italian seasoning, salt, garlic powder, onion powder, pepper and chili flakes, if using. Stir until the chicken is coated in the seasonings.

2. Add the olive oil to the Instant Pot. Press "Sauté" and wait 1 to 2 minutes for the olive oil to get hot. Add the chicken and cook for 4 to 5 minutes, stirring occasionally. Press "Cancel" to exit the sauté function.

3. Add the fusilli pasta on top of the chicken. Then, pour the marinara sauce and water on top. DO NOT STIR.

4. Secure the lid. Press the "Pressure Cook" button until the display light is under "HIGH" and use the "-/+" button to adjust the time to 5 minutes. Be sure the valve on top is set to sealing.

5. While the pasta cooks, make the breadcrumb topping. In a small frying pan over medium heat, add the olive oil. When hot, add the Panko breadcrumbs and the garlic. Cook until golden, for about 3 minutes. Remove from heat and stir in the Parmesan cheese and parsley. Set the breadcrumbs aside in a bowl.

6. Once the pasta is done, allow the pressure to naturally release for 5 minutes. Quick release any of the remaining pressure and once the pin drops, remove the lid. Give the pasta a good stir. Add the mozzarella and Parmesan cheese on top and replace the lid until the cheese melts over the pasta, for 5 additional minutes. Serve with the toasted breadcrumbs on top, fresh basil or parsley and more Parmesan cheese.

TAWNIE'S TIP: A lot of my recipes use Italian seasoning but if you don't have any, feel free to use a combination of dried basil, oregano, rosemary, parsley and thyme.

SAUSAGE AND SPINACH GNOCCHI

YIELD: 4 SERVINGS
TOTAL TIME: 25 MINUTES

1 tbsp (15 ml) olive oil

1 small yellow onion, finely diced

2 cloves garlic, minced

1 lb (454 g) Italian sausage, hot or sweet

1 tsp fennel seed

1 tsp Italian seasoning

¾ cup (180 ml) chicken broth

1 (1-lb [454-g]) package potato gnocchi

1 (15-oz [425-g]) can crushed tomatoes

2 cups (60 g) baby spinach, chopped

1 cup (100 g) finely grated Parmesan cheese

½ oz (14 g) fresh basil, chopped

Salt and pepper, to taste

Garnish
Parmesan cheese

Fresh basil

Pillowy soft gnocchi blanketed in a flavorful red sauce filled with Italian sausage and spinach screams quintessential comfort. This meal comes together in less than 30 minutes, and I know it will be making its way to your regular dinner rotation. Serve with a generous dusting of Parmesan cheese and aromatic basil.

1. Add the olive oil to the bottom of the Instant Pot. Press "Sauté" and once the oil is hot, add in the onion and garlic. Sauté for 2 to 3 minutes. Then, add in the Italian sausage and break up the meat with a wooden spoon until it is no longer pink. Add the fennel seed and Italian seasoning and stir.

2. Pour in the chicken broth to deglaze the bottom and scrape any brown bits at the bottom of the pot. Add the gnocchi and the crushed tomatoes and DO NOT STIR.

3. Secure the lid and press "Cancel" to exit the sauté mode. Press the "Pressure Cook" button until the display light is under "HIGH" and use the "-/+" button to adjust the time to 2 minutes. Be sure the valve on top is set to sealing.

4. Once the gnocchi are done, allow the pressure to naturally release for 2 to 3 minutes. Quick release any of the remaining pressure and once the pin drops, remove the lid.

5. Press "Sauté" again and adjust to sauté on low. Add in the spinach, Parmesan cheese and basil. Stir to combine and let the gnocchi simmer, stirring occasionally. The sauce will thicken as it sits. Taste and add salt or pepper as desired and serve with additional Parmesan cheese and basil on top.

TAWNIE'S TIP: I love substituting chopped kale in place of spinach for a slightly different texture and taste!

LINGUINE ALLA CARBONARA

YIELD: 2-4 SERVINGS
TOTAL TIME: 30 MINUTES

For the pasta

8 oz (227 g) linguine pasta, uncooked

2½ cups (600 ml) filtered water

2 tbsp (28 g) unsalted butter

½ tsp kosher salt

Reserved pasta water

1 tbsp (15 ml) olive oil

For the sauce

2 tbsp (28 g) unsalted butter

2 tbsp (30 g) olive oil

4 strips thick-cut bacon, chopped into small pieces

1 shallot, minced

2 cloves garlic, minced

2 large eggs, room temperature

4 oz (113 g) freshly grated Pecorino Romano cheese

Garnish

Black pepper, coarsely ground

Pecorino Romano cheese

TAWNIE'S TIPS:

- To make the bacon easier to cut, freeze it for about an hour prior to using it.

- Traditionally, carbonara is made with guanciale so of course use guanciale if you prefer.

Don't let the simple ingredients list fool you. This linguine carbonara is far from basic! It's a decadent dish and the noodles are enveloped in the most amazing creamy, silky sauce, yet no cream is added to this pasta. Use my tips and recommendations to prevent the sauce from curdling, because there is nothing worse than overcooking the eggs and ending up with scrambled eggs and pasta. You want the eggs to cook perfectly to reach a custardy consistency that creates a tangle of comfort and glazes the linguine beautifully. You'll be impressed at how flavorful this carbonara is and you'll be wanting to double the recipe next time you make it!

1. Break the linguine noodles in half and place them in the Instant Pot in a crisscross pattern. Pour the water on top. Press the linguine down gently so they are mainly submerged in water but DO NOT STIR. Add the butter and salt on top.

2. Secure the lid in place with the steam vent sealed. Press the "Pressure Cook" button until the display light is under "HIGH" and use the "-/+" button to adjust the time until the display reads 7 minutes. Once the timer sounds, let the pot sit undisturbed to allow the pressure to naturally release for 5 minutes. Then, release any of the remaining pressure. Once the pin drops, remove the lid.

3. Reserve all the starchy pasta water (about ½ cup [120 ml]). Toss the noodles in a large bowl with olive oil to coat so they don't stick together. Set aside to allow the pasta to cool slightly before adding in the egg mixture so the eggs don't turn into something like scrambled eggs. Press "Cancel."

4. To add the sauce, press "Sauté." Add the butter and olive oil and once hot, add the bacon and cook until rendered, 6 to 7 minutes. Add the shallot and garlic and cook for 2 minutes. Press "Cancel."

5. Whisk together the eggs and Pecorino Romano cheese in a small mixing bowl.

6. Add the shallot and bacon mixture to the linguine in the large bowl. Then, begin to whisk the egg and Pecorino Romano mixture in. Lastly, begin to slowly whisk in the reserved pasta water, only adding a little at a time until desired creaminess is reached. The sauce should thicken to a creamy, silky consistency. You may not use all the water and that is okay. Garnish with pepper and Pecorino Romano and enjoy immediately.

Meaty Mains

Whether you're craving beef, chicken, sausage or fish, this chapter has something for you! These recipes can be made effortlessly and each dish will simultaneously look and feel fancier than it really is. For instance, my take on Beef Braciole (page 46) sounds intimidating, but it's rather quite simple and you end up with a wonderful main dish in a beautifully flavored, wine-infused pasta sauce. These meaty mains are comfort food classics and they are 1,000 percent worth having in your repertoire.

I didn't use to be a very savvy meat cooker. My husband takes over when it comes to barbecuing or making tender, slow-cooked meats. But things changed when I started using the Instant Pot more and more. Recipes such as Beef Ragu Pappardelle (page 38) are no longer intimidating and being able to cook a Whole Italian Chicken (page 55) without having to heat up the house has become a total game changer.

It doesn't matter if you're new to the world of Instant Pot cooking or if you're a seasoned pressure-cooking pro, these meaty main recipes are all approachable. It is always part of my mission as a recipe developer to make realistic and approachable recipes for all cooks alike.

I had so much fun developing these recipes for you in this chapter. I hope at least one meal (if not all!) lures you in and becomes a favorite dinner for you and your family.

FLORENTINE CHICKEN MEATBALLS

For the meatballs

1 lb (454 g) ground chicken

1 large egg, lightly beaten

½ cup (50 g) finely grated Parmesan cheese

½ cup (54 g) Italian breadcrumbs

1 cup (30 g) finely chopped fresh spinach

2 tbsp (30 ml) olive oil

1 tbsp (4 g) chopped fresh parsley

1 tbsp (3 g) chopped fresh basil

½ tsp garlic powder

½ tsp onion powder

½ tsp kosher salt

¼ tsp freshly ground black pepper

For the sauce

24 oz (680 g) jarred marinara sauce

⅔ cup (160 ml) filtered water

Garnish

Mozzarella cheese, shredded

Freshly grated Parmesan cheese

Fresh basil

Fresh parsley

Trust me when I say these chicken meatballs are far from boring. Want to know my secret? Add olive oil! Since ground chicken lacks fat, it's important to imbue them with moisture and fat and a little olive oil helps make these meatballs ultra-juicy and flavorful. These perfectly seasoned and tender Florentine Chicken Meatballs are best served on a mound of your favorite pasta smothered in marinara and topped with fresh mozzarella. You need to put these on your menu tonight!

1. To make the chicken meatballs, mix the ground chicken, egg, Parmesan cheese, Italian breadcrumbs, fresh spinach, olive oil, parsley, basil, garlic powder, onion powder, salt and pepper in a large bowl until combined.

2. Line a rimmed baking sheet with parchment paper or a silicone baking mat. Form into meatballs using a 2 tablespoon (30-ml) cookie scoop. Use a little olive oil on your hands if the meatballs feel sticky. Place the meatballs on the prepared baking sheet and continue shaping until all the meat is used.

3. Pour the marinara sauce and water into the Instant Pot. Whisk to combine. Gently place the meatballs in the Instant Pot, being careful not to jam or flatten them as you layer them in. Place the lid on and be sure the valve on top is set to sealing. Press the "Pressure Cook" button until the display light is under "HIGH" and use the "-/+" button to adjust the time to 5 minutes.

4. Once the timer sounds, let the pot sit undisturbed to allow the pressure to naturally release for 10 minutes. Then, quick release any of the remaining pressure. Once the pin drops, remove the lid.

5. Carefully spoon out the meatballs. Enjoy warm with your favorite pasta and garnish with your favorite toppings: shredded mozzarella cheese, Parmesan cheese, basil, parsley, etc.

TAWNIE'S TIPS:

- Make these a day in advance! Form the meatballs and place on a parchment paper-lined baking sheet. Cover and place in the refrigerator until you're ready to make dinner.

- It's always fun to serve as an appetizer with toothpicks and red sauce for dipping.

BEEF RAGU PAPPARDELLE

YIELD: 6 SERVINGS

TOTAL TIME: 1 HOUR 15 MINUTES

1½–2 lb (681–907 g) chuck roast, boneless

1½ tsp (9 g) kosher salt

¾ tsp black pepper

2 tbsp (30 ml) olive oil, divided

1 small yellow onion, finely diced

2 large carrots, peeled and finely diced

3 ribs celery, finely chopped

½ bulb fennel, finely diced

4 cloves garlic, minced

1 cup (240 ml) beef broth

½ cup (120 ml) cabernet sauvignon or other red wine

1 (28-oz [794-g]) can crushed tomatoes

3 tbsp (48 g) tomato paste

1 tsp dried thyme

1 tsp dried oregano

1 tsp fresh rosemary, chopped

2 bay leaves

12 oz (340 g) pappardelle pasta

Garnish

Flat leaf Italian parsley

Parmesan cheese

TAWNIE'S TIP: I love this ragu over 20-Minute Parmesan Polenta too (recipe on page 121)!

This beef ragu is the definition of a warming meal with a tomato-based sauce, fall-apart tender beef and aromatic herbs. This recipe is hearty and flavorful but made in a fraction of the time compared to the slow cooker version. You'll love that it's an effortless meal and instantly gives you all the cozy, feel-good vibes! Pile it high on top of big, twirly pappardelle pasta and garnish generously with fresh parsley and Parmesan cheese.

1. Cut the chuck into about 4 or 5 pieces or about 3-inch (7.5-cm) chunks. Pat them dry with a paper towel and season both sides with salt and pepper.

2. Add 1 tablespoon (15 ml) of olive oil to the bottom of the Instant Pot. Press "Sauté" and once the oil is hot, add the beef in. Cook for about 2 to 3 minutes on each side and then set aside on a plate.

3. Add the remaining tablespoon (15 ml) of olive oil to the pot. Add in the onion, carrots, celery, fennel and garlic. Cook, stirring occasionally, for about 7 minutes or until the vegetables are softened and fragrant. Pour in the beef broth and red wine and allow everything to simmer for 5 minutes.

4. Pour in the crushed tomatoes, tomato paste, thyme, oregano, rosemary and bay leaves. Stir to combine and then place the beef into the pot. Secure the lid and press "Cancel" to exit the sauté mode. Press the "Pressure Cook" button until the display light is under "HIGH" and use the "-/+" button to adjust the time to 40 minutes. Be sure the valve on top is set to sealing.

5. Meanwhile, bring a large pot of salted water to boil over medium-high heat. Cook the pappardelle pasta (or pasta shape of choice) according to the package directions. Drain and set aside. Once the timer sounds, let the Instant Pot sit undisturbed to allow the pressure to naturally release for 10 minutes. Then, quick release any of the remaining pressure. Once the pin drops, remove the lid.

6. Discard the bay leaves and shred the beef. Stir shredded beef into the sauce. Add the cooked pasta into the sauce or serve the beef ragu over the pasta and garnish with fresh parsley and Parmesan cheese.

20-MINUTE CREAMY CHICKEN MARSALA

YIELD: 4 SERVINGS

TOTAL TIME: 20 MINUTES

¼ cup (31 g) all-purpose flour

1 tsp kosher salt

½ tsp Italian seasoning

¼ tsp black pepper

1½ lb (682 g) boneless, skinless chicken breasts, butterflied and halved

1½ tbsp (23 ml) olive oil

2 tbsp (28 g) unsalted butter

1 shallot, minced

8 oz (227 g) baby portabella mushrooms, sliced

3 cloves garlic, minced

¾ cup (180 ml) dry Marsala wine (see Tip)

¾ cup (180 ml) chicken broth

2 tsp (5 g) cornstarch + 2 tsp (10 ml) water

¼ cup (60 ml) heavy cream

2 tbsp (8 g) fresh flat leaf Italian parsley, chopped

1 tsp fresh thyme

Salt and pepper, to taste

8 oz (226 g) pasta of choice, cooked

Garnish

Fresh parsley

I've lost count of the number of times I've made this Italian classic. Everyone always loves it and this version especially is simple and quick to make. Butter, garlic and meaty mushrooms join juicy, tender chicken in a rich Marsala wine sauce slightly thickened with heavy cream.

1. Mix the flour, salt, Italian seasoning and pepper in a shallow bowl. Dredge the cut chicken halves in the flour mixture and shake off any excess. Add the olive oil to the bottom of the Instant Pot. Press "Sauté" and once the oil is hot, add the chicken in, working in batches to avoid overcrowding the pot. Brown the chicken, cooking for 2 to 3 minutes on each side and then set aside on a plate.

2. Add the butter and once melted, add the shallot, mushrooms and garlic. Cook, stirring frequently so nothing sticks to the bottom, for 3 to 4 minutes.

3. Deglaze the bottom of the pan with the Marsala wine, scraping up any browned bits. Allow to simmer for 2 to 3 minutes. Then, pour in the chicken broth. Press "Cancel" to exit the sauté mode. Add the chicken back in, and submerge under the liquid.

4. Secure the lid. Press the "Pressure Cook" button until the display light is under "HIGH" and use the "-/+" button to adjust the time to 5 minutes. Be sure the valve on top is set to sealing. Once the timer sounds, quick release the pressure. Remove the lid once the pin drops.

5. Switch back to the sauté mode again. Remove the chicken breasts and set them on a plate. Stir together the cornstarch and water and whisk it into the sauce to thicken. Add in the heavy cream and fresh herbs. Stir. Press "Cancel" to exit the sauté mode. Add the chicken in. Taste the sauce and add more salt and pepper to taste. Serve with your favorite pasta and garnish with parsley.

TAWNIE'S TIP: I recommend using a dry Marsala wine, as opposed to a sweet one. Sweet Marsala is used for desserts and won't work well for this recipe. Marsala wine is a fortified wine made in Sicily and used to create nutty, rich caramelized sauces making it a perfect companion for Chicken Marsala.

WEEKNIGHT SAUSAGE AND PEPPERS

YIELD: 4-5 SERVINGS

TOTAL TIME: 35 MINUTES

½ cup (120 ml) beef broth

1 (14.5-oz [411-g]) petite diced tomatoes in juices

¾ cup (198 g) passata (tomato puree)

1 tsp Italian seasoning

1 tsp garlic powder

1 tsp onion powder

1 tsp kosher salt

½ tsp black pepper

1 lb (454 g) mild or sweet Italian sausage links in casing (5 links)

3 bell peppers, sliced (1 yellow, 1 red, 1 orange)

1 small yellow onion, sliced

Buns, risotto or pasta, for serving

This is a one-pot, dump and start, low-effort meal that's ideal for weeknights and when you're craving something warm and comforting. It's packed with sweet Italian sausage, colorful and tender bell peppers and tomatoes. I love this as-is or loaded onto a bun or served over pasta. This is a great dish for meal prep too—just chop all the bell peppers and onion ahead of time so that when you're ready to make dinner, you can immediately dump everything in the Instant Pot and start!

1. Add the broth, diced tomatoes, passata, Italian seasoning, garlic powder, onion powder, salt and pepper into the Instant Pot. Then add the sausages in and top with the sliced peppers and onion. DO NOT STIR.

2. Secure the lid. Press the "Pressure Cook" button until the display light is under "HIGH" and use the "-/+" button to adjust the time to 20 minutes. Be sure the valve on top is set to sealing. Once the timer sounds, quick release the pressure. Remove the lid once the pin drops. Give everything a big stir. The sauce will be relatively thin, so you can thicken with tomato paste if preferred.

3. Serve the sausages and peppers on buns or slice the sausage and serve over risotto or pasta.

TAWNIE'S TIP: Feeling cheesy?! Place the cooked sausages and peppers into an oven-safe baking dish and top with shredded mozzarella. Place under the broiler for a couple minutes until the cheese is golden brown and bubbly. YUM!

OUR FAVORITE BEEF MEATBALLS

YIELD: 20 MEATBALLS

TOTAL TIME: 1 HOUR

For the meatballs

1 lb (454 g) ground beef

⅓ cup (45 g) Italian breadcrumbs

¼ cup (40 g) white onion, grated or finely chopped

1 large egg, lightly beaten

2 tbsp (30 g) ketchup

1 tbsp (15 g) Dijon mustard

2 cloves garlic, minced

2 tsp (10 ml) Worcestershire sauce

1 tsp dried parsley

1 tsp kosher salt

½ tsp dried oregano

For the sauce

32 oz (900 g) jarred marinara sauce

⅔ cup (160 ml) water

Garnish

Parmesan cheese

Fresh basil, chopped

Fresh flat leaf Italian parsley

This recipe gets me like, really excited. I mean, what's not to love about mouthwateringly juicy, flavorful meatballs that are a breeze to bring together? These meatballs are on our regular meal rotation and I know they'll become a weeknight favorite in your home too. Serve them as an appetizer with lots of freshly grated Parmesan on top, over your favorite pasta or my husband's favorite: loaded on a meatball sub.

1. To make the meatballs, mix the ground beef, Italian breadcrumbs, white onion, egg, ketchup, Dijon mustard, garlic, Worcestershire sauce, dried parsley, salt and dried oregano in a large bowl until combined.

2. Line a rimmed baking sheet with parchment paper or a silicone baking mat. Form into meatballs using a 2-tablespoon (30-ml) cookie scoop. Place the meatballs on the prepared baking sheet and continue shaping until all the meat is used. This will make approximately 20 meatballs. Place the meatballs in the fridge for 30 minutes (this makes them easier to handle and helps them keep their shape).

3. Pour the marinara sauce and water into the Instant Pot. Whisk to combine. Gently place the chilled meatballs in the Instant Pot, being careful not to jam or flatten them as you layer them in. Secure the lid. Press the "Pressure Cook" button until the display light is under "HIGH" and use the "-/+" button to adjust the time to 7 minutes. Be sure the valve on top is set to sealing.

4. Once the timer sounds, let the pot sit undisturbed to allow the pressure to naturally release for 5 minutes. Then, quick release any of the remaining pressure. Remove the lid once the pin drops.

5. Enjoy with your favorite pasta and garnish with your favorite toppings such as freshly grated Parmesan cheese, basil, parsley, etc.

TAWNIE'S TIPS:

- Substitute ground beef for ground turkey if preferred.
- If your Instant Pot is signaling the "BURN" notice, more liquid may be needed. Adding more water can help.
- Rinse the marinara jar with a little swish of water to get all the yummy sauce that has stuck to the bottom and sides of the jar and pour it in the Instant Pot too!

BEEF BRACIOLE

YIELD: 4 SERVINGS
TOTAL TIME: 1 HOUR
10 MINUTES

For the braciole

1–1 ¼ lb (454–568 g) thinly sliced top round, skirt steak, or flank steak

Pinch of salt and pepper

3 oz (85 g) prosciutto (4 thin slices)

½ cup (50 g) freshly shredded Parmesan cheese

½ cup (54 g) Italian breadcrumbs

½ cup (35 g) baby portabella mushrooms, finely diced

3 cloves garlic, pressed

⅓ cup (21 g) fresh flat leaf Italian parsley, finely chopped

¼ cup (6 g) fresh basil, finely chopped

1 egg, beaten

¼ tsp kosher salt

⅛ tsp black pepper

3 tbsp (45 ml) olive oil

Say hello to yummy, thin slices of tender beef stuffed with a savory breadcrumb filling and cooked in a hearty red wine–infused sauce. *Braciole* in Italian means a slice of meat wrapped around a filling. This Italian classic has countless variations but whatever way you make it, it's always a favorite. Enjoy this meal with a well-deserved glass of wine!

1. You'll need 4 slices of meat, each slice approximately 6 to 7 inches (15–17 cm) long and 3 to 4 (8–10 cm) inches wide. Lay the slices of top round on a clean surface and pound them flat with a meat tenderizer until they are about ⅛ inch (0.3 cm) thick. Season both sides with a pinch of salt and pepper. Place one slice of prosciutto on top of each slice of beef.

2. Prepare the breadcrumb filling in a medium-sized mixing bowl by combining the Parmesan cheese, breadcrumbs, mushrooms, garlic, parsley, basil, egg, salt and pepper. Mix well until it comes together. Evenly distribute the filling among the beef and press it into the meat to help compact it, about ⅓ cup filling in each. Carefully begin to roll the meat jelly roll-style, beginning at the short end. Repeat with the remaining slices. Secure the rolls closed with butcher's twine.

(continued)

For the sauce

½ cup (120 ml) beef broth, plus a splash

1 small yellow onion, diced small

2 large carrots, diced small

2 ribs celery, diced small

4 cloves garlic, minced

½ cup (120 ml) cabernet sauvignon or other red wine

1 (28-oz [794-g]) can crushed tomatoes

2 tbsp (32 g) tomato paste

2 bay leaves

1 tbsp (2 g) fresh oregano, chopped

Garnish

2 tbsp (8 g) fresh flat leaf Italian parsley, chopped

2 tbsp (4 g) fresh basil, chopped

Parmesan cheese, finely grated

3. Add the oil to the Instant Pot. Press "Sauté" and once the oil is hot, begin to sear each braciole just until browned on each side. Remove and set aside on a plate. Deglaze the bottom of the pot with a small splash of beef broth, being sure to scrape up any browned bits left behind.

4. Add the onion, carrots, celery and garlic. Sauté for 5 minutes, stirring occasionally. Add the red wine and let it simmer for 3 to 4 minutes. Then, add the beef broth and crushed tomatoes and stir. Nestle the braciole into the pot. Add the tomato paste and bay leaves on top, but DO NOT STIR. Press "Cancel" to exit the sauté mode.

5. Secure the lid. Press the "Pressure Cook" button until the display light is under "HIGH" and use the "-/+" button to adjust the time to 30 minutes. Be sure the valve on top is set to sealing.

6. Once the timer sounds, let the pot sit undisturbed to allow the pressure to naturally release for 10 minutes. Then, quick release any of the remaining pressure. Remove the lid once the pin drops. Stir in the fresh oregano. Remove the bay leaves from the sauce. Serve the braciole hot along with the red sauce and garnish with parsley, basil and Parmesan cheese. Be sure to remove the butcher's twine before cutting into the braciole!

TAWNIE'S TIPS:

- Is your Instant pot getting the "BURN" message? Be sure to not skip the deglazing step after you brown the braciole.

- This recipe makes a good amount of sauce. Feel free to serve any leftovers over your favorite cooked pasta or the 20-Minute Parmesan Polenta (page 121) .

CHICKEN CACCIATORE

YIELD: 4-6 SERVINGS
TOTAL TIME: 40 MINUTES

4–6 (1–1.5 lb [454–681 g]) boneless, skinless chicken thighs

¼ cup (31 g) all-purpose flour

1 tsp kosher salt

¼ tsp black pepper

2 tbsp (30 ml) olive oil

½ small white onion, diced

1 large carrot, diced

1 red bell pepper, seeded and sliced into strips

1 yellow bell pepper, seeded and sliced into strips

8 oz (227 g) baby portabella mushrooms, sliced

2 cloves garlic, minced

½ cup (120 ml) pinot grigio, sauvignon blanc or a dry chardonnay

½ cup (120 ml) chicken broth

1 (15-oz [425-g]) can crushed tomatoes in puree

1 (6-oz [170-g]) can tomato paste

1 tbsp (15 ml) balsamic vinegar

¼ cup (15 g) fresh flat leaf Italian parsley, chopped

2 tbsp (4 g) fresh thyme

1 sprig rosemary, chopped

½ tsp red pepper chili flakes

This dish is flavorful, hearty and full of tender, pull-apart chicken swimming in a sweet, veggie-loaded sauce. It's a comforting dinner infused with lots of fresh herbs and simply an Italian classic. It's versatile enough to be able to add whatever veggies you have on hand, so feel free to change it up based on what you have stocked in your kitchen. It's a meal adults and children alike will love, making it the perfect Sunday night recipe.

1. Pat the chicken thighs dry. Whisk together the flour, salt and pepper in a shallow bowl. Dredge the chicken in the flour and set aside on a plate.

2. Add the olive oil to the Instant Pot. Press "Sauté" and wait a minute or two for the olive oil to get hot. Brown the chicken thighs for 1 to 2 minutes on each side, working in batches as needed. Set the chicken aside.

3. Add the onion, carrot, bell peppers and mushrooms. Add a touch more of olive oil, if needed. Sauté for 5 minutes or until vegetables begin to soften. Add the garlic and stir for 30 seconds to combine. Deglaze with the white wine. Allow the wine to simmer for about 2 to 3 minutes.

4. Pour in the chicken broth. Press "Cancel" to exit the sauté mode. Add the chicken thighs back into the pot. Add the crushed tomatoes, tomato paste, balsamic vinegar, herbs and chili flakes on top and DO NOT STIR.

(continued)

12 oz (340 g) pasta of choice, cooked

Garnish

Fresh basil

Flat leaf Italian parsley

Parmesan cheese

5. Secure the lid. Press the "Pressure Cook" button until the display light is under "HIGH" and use the "–/+" button to adjust the time to 8 minutes. Be sure the valve on top is set to sealing. Once the timer sounds, let the pot sit undisturbed to allow the pressure to naturally release for 10 minutes. Then, quick release any of the remaining pressure. Remove the lid once the pin drops. Give it a good stir to combine.

6. Press "Sauté" and choose the less mode and summer the sauce for 3 to 5 minutes to thicken. Serve with your pasta of choice and garnish with fresh basil, parsley and Parmesan.

TAWNIE'S TIPS:

- Pssst! Don't skip out on dredging the chicken in flour. The flour helps act as a thickening agent to create a velvety tomato sauce.

- If you'd like to add in capers or kalamata olives, add them in Step 4 after the crushed tomatoes.

SALMON PICCATA

YIELD: 2 SERVINGS

TOTAL TIME: 25 MINUTES

For the salmon

1 cup (240 ml) water

2 (5–6 oz [142–171 g]) skinless salmon filets

1 tsp kosher salt

A few grinds freshly ground black pepper

2 tbsp (28 g) salted butter

1 lemon, sliced

For the sauce

½ cup (120 ml) chicken broth

¼ cup (60 ml) sauvignon blanc or a full body chardonnay

¼ cup (60 ml) lemon juice

1 tbsp (6 g) lemon zest

¼ cup (30 g) capers, drained

3 cloves garlic, minced

2 tbsp (28 g) salted butter

1 tsp fresh flat leaf Italian parsley, chopped

½ tsp dried basil

½ tsp dried oregano

½ tsp kosher salt

Freshly ground black pepper, to taste

2 tsp (5 g) cornstarch + 2 tsp (10 ml) water

8 oz (226 g) pasta of choice, cooked

Piccata has got all the right elements: simplicity, great flavor, lightness and of course, the best tangy lemon-butter sauce studded with briny capers. The Instant Pot helps create a succulent, flaky salmon in just 3 minutes and after that, all you need to do is bring together the sauce. This restuarant-quality meal made in less than 30 minutes will soon be a firm favorite in your house.

1. Pour the water into the Instant Pot. Spray the trivet with nonstick spray then place it on top of the water. Pat the salmon filets dry with paper towels and then season with salt and pepper. Place the salmon on the trivet in a single layer, not overlapping. Add 1 tablespoon (14 g) of butter on top of each filet along with a slice of lemon.

2. Secure the lid and be sure the valve on top is set to sealing. Press the "Pressure Cook" button until the display light is under "HIGH" and use the "-/+" button to adjust the time to 3 minutes. Once the timer sounds, quick release the pressure and once the pin drops, remove the lid. Carefully remove the salmon and trivet and set aside on a plate. Discard the water and place the pot back into the base to make the sauce.

3. Press "Cancel" and then press "Sauté." Add in the chicken broth, wine, lemon juice, lemon zest, capers and garlic. Bring to a simmer for 2 to 3 minutes. Then whisk in the butter. Add in the fresh parsley, dried basil and oregano, salt and pepper and stir to combine. To thicken the sauce, whisk in the cornstarch and water. If the sauce is too thick, stir in more chicken broth until the desired consistency is reached. Taste and adjust seasonings, if needed.

4. Spoon the sauce over the salmon and serve with pasta of choice. Enjoy!

TAWNIE'S TIPS:

- The quick release function is ideal for delicate seafood recipes, like this salmon. Be sure to quick release the pressure especially for this recipe so the salmon doesn't become dry or tough.

- If using frozen salmon, cook at 5 minutes HIGH pressure instead of 3.

WHOLE ITALIAN CHICKEN

YIELD: 6-8 SERVINGS

TOTAL TIME: 1 HOUR 10 MINUTES

1 whole (4.5-lb [2-kg]) chicken

1½ tbsp (7 g) Italian seasoning

2 tsp (6 g) garlic powder

2 tsp (6 g) onion powder

1 tbsp (17 g) kosher salt

¼ tsp black pepper

3 tbsp (45 ml) olive oil

½ lemon

3 sprigs fresh rosemary

3 sprigs fresh thyme

1 cup (240 ml) chicken broth

For the gravy

Drippings

4 tbsp (57 g) butter

¼ cup (31 g) all-purpose flour

1 cup (240 ml) chicken broth

1 tbsp (2 g) fresh rosemary, chopped

1 tbsp (2 g) fresh thyme, chopped

Salt and pepper, to taste

TAWNIE'S TIP: A simple rule to follow for figuring out the cook time for a whole chicken is 6 minutes at HIGH pressure per pound of chicken. So, if your chicken is smaller or a bit larger, you can use this easy guide.

No turning on the oven and getting the entire house hot when you can make a whole chicken right in your Instant Pot! It's magically tender and juicy, unbelievably easy to make and turns out perfect every single time. If you'd like crispy skin, you can pop it under the broiler in the oven for a minute or two. Serve for a Sunday supper with mashed potatoes or make for meal prep for the week.

1. Remove the chicken from the fridge and let the chicken come to room temperature for 30 minutes directly before cooking. Pat the entire chicken dry with paper towels and remove giblets from inside the chicken.

2. In a small bowl, combine the Italian seasoning, garlic powder, onion powder, salt and pepper. Then, mix in the olive oil. Spread the seasonings all over the chicken. Then, stuff the chicken with half of a lemon, rosemary and thyme.

3. Pour 1 cup (240 ml) of chicken broth into the Instant Pot and then place the trivet down. Carefully set the chicken, breast side up, onto the trivet.

4. Secure the lid and be sure the valve on top is set to sealing. Press the "Pressure Cook" button until the display light is under "HIGH" and use the "-/+" button to adjust the time to 27 minutes. Once the timer sounds, let the pot sit undisturbed to allow the pressure to naturally release for at least 15 minutes. I usually let it sit for 40 minutes before removing the lid for the most tender and moist results.

5. Place the chicken on a foil-lined baking sheet and broil the chicken until the skin is golden brown. Allow the chicken to rest for 10 to 15 minutes before slicing and enjoying.

6. To make the gravy, pour the chicken drippings into a measuring cup and skim and strain any impurities. Press "Sauté" on the Instant Pot and melt the butter, whisk in the flour and cook, whisking frequently until the flour turns a light brown color and smells slightly nutty, 2 to 3 minutes. Slowly begin to whisk in the broth and season with chopped rosemary, thyme, salt and pepper. Simmer to thicken and serve over the chicken.

BLOW-YOUR-MIND ITALIAN MEATLOAF AND POTATOES

YIELD: 6–8 SERVINGS
TOTAL TIME: 1 HOUR

For the meatloaf

2 lbs (908 g) ground beef (or 1 lb [454 g] beef, 1 lb [454 g] Italian sausage)

2 large eggs, beaten

6 cloves garlic, minced

½ white onion, grated

1 tbsp (5 g) dried basil

½ large red bell pepper, finely chopped

¼ cup (15 g) fresh flat leaf Italian parsley, finely chopped

2 tsp (12 g) kosher salt

½ tsp black pepper

1 cup (100 g) grated Parmesan cheese

1 cup (108 g) Italian breadcrumbs

1 tbsp (15 ml) Worcestershire sauce

1 tbsp (15 ml) balsamic vinegar

For the meatloaf topping

1 cup (225 g) marinara sauce, divided

1 cup (112 g) shredded mozzarella

You'll love that this is an all-in-one meal streamlined right in the Instant Pot. The fact that you can whip up the mashed potatoes and the meatloaf in the same pot is mind blowing and you'll soon be obsessed! Hello creamy Parmesan-doused potatoes and tender meatloaf seasoned with lots of garlic and herbs. Humble ingredients, made comforting and downright scrumptious. Any leftovers will make for great meatloaf sandwiches throughout the week!

1. Spray the bottom of the Instant Pot with nonstick cooking spray. Add the potatoes into the pot with the water. Gently place the trivet on top of the potatoes.

2. To make the meatloaf, mix the ground beef, eggs, garlic, white onion, dried basil, red bell pepper, parsley, salt, pepper, Parmesan cheese, breadcrumbs, Worcestershire sauce and balsamic vinegar in a large mixing bowl. Transfer to a sheet of nonstick aluminum foil and shape into a rectangle or a circle, whatever you feel will fit best in your Instant Pot. Spread about ⅓ cup (75 g) of the marinara sauce all over the top of the meatloaf. Fold up the sides of the foil to create a little boat and this also helps to create "handles" or a foil sling.

3. Carefully set the meatloaf with the foil sling on top of the trivet. Secure the lid and be sure the valve on top is set to sealing. Press the "Pressure Cook" button until the display light is under "HIGH" and use the "-/+" button to adjust the time to 28 minutes. Once the timer sounds, let the pot sit undisturbed to allow the pressure to naturally release for 10 minutes.

4. Release any of the remaining pressure and once the pin drops, remove the lid. Discard some of the water/drippings that have collected around the meatloaf (pro tip: a baster works well to remove the drippings). Carefully remove the meatloaf from the Instant Pot using oven mitts and transfer to a foil-lined baking sheet. Top with the remaining marinara sauce and mozzarella cheese. Heat the oven to broil and broil until the cheese is melted and bubbly, for 2 to 3 minutes.

For the potatoes

24 oz (680 g) baby Yukon gold potatoes, quartered

1 cup (240 ml) water

1 tsp kosher salt

¼ cup (60 ml) whole milk

¼ cup (60 ml) sour cream

3 cloves garlic, finely grated

½ cup (50 g) freshly grated Parmesan cheese

1 tsp dried basil

½ tsp fresh rosemary, chopped

½ tsp fresh thyme, chopped

2 tbsp (28 g) unsalted butter

5. For the potatoes, drain the water from the potatoes and add the potatoes back into the pot. Add in the salt, whole milk, sour cream, garlic, Parmesan cheese, dried basil, rosemary, thyme and butter and mash to combine. Taste and adjust seasonings as desired.

TAWNIE'S TIP: If you want to keep your potatoes whole, feel free! Instead of mashing, add butter and herbs and stir to coat the potatoes for a simple, yet flavorful creamy potato side dish.

Meatless Mains

This chapter is a whole mood filled with some of my favorite meatless pastas. I'm taking it back to basics with this chapter and not overcomplicating ingredient lists or directions—just big flavor meals that are quick and easy to make and of course, they're vegetarian!

You'll find plenty of plant-powered options, but they are far from boring. Like my Orzo and Vegetable Stuffed Peppers (page 78). Tender bell peppers get stuffed to the brim with quick-to-cook orzo, mushrooms, broccoli and zucchini. They are an ideal dinner option any night of the week and our whole family, toddler included, loves this one. There is also a lot of creamy magic happening in these meatless pastas. I have to warn you about the 3 Cheese Italian Mac and Cheese (page 65) because it is dangerously good and you literally won't be able to stop eating it. And if you're looking for something light, refreshing and extremely easy, my Quick and Easy Bruschetta Pasta (page 77) is just that. It is seemingly fancy, but we all need food to be easy sometimes.

These crave-able pastas are going to make you come back for more and more and then yes, even more. I just can't say enough good things about these yummy recipes and especially can't wait for your tastebuds to adore these flavor-packed, pasta-loving, veggie-loaded mains!

EGGPLANT ARRABBIATA PASTA

1 large eggplant

2½ tsp (15 g) kosher salt, divided

1 tbsp (15 ml) olive oil

½ yellow onion, finely diced

4 cloves garlic, minced

3½ cups (840 ml) water

1 (15-oz [425-g]) can crushed tomatoes

1 (15-oz [425-g]) can tomato sauce

12 oz (340 g) tri-color rotini, uncooked

1 tbsp (15 g) sugar

1 tsp Italian seasoning

¾ tsp red pepper chili flakes (or less if desired)

Black pepper, to taste

Garnish
Finely grated Parmesan cheese

Fresh basil

To many people, there's nothing extremely exciting about eggplant besides maybe eggplant Parmesan. But when cooked in a certain way like in this arrabbiata pasta, it reaches new heights. Arrabbiata is a spicy marinara sauce that means "angry" thanks to the red pepper chili flakes. I've amped up the traditional recipe with onion, Italian seasonings, fresh basil and a little sugar to balance out the acidity from the tomatoes. This recipe is not complicated, has a basic ingredient list and is a delicious meatless option. Spice up your weeknight meal with this pasta and *buon appetito!*

1. Wash and slice the eggplant into ½-inch (1.3-cm)-thick slices. Lay the eggplant on a paper towel–lined baking sheet (or simply place the slices in a colander) and sprinkle the eggplant slices on both sides with 2 teaspoons (12 g) of the salt. Let the eggplant sweat out the excess beads of moisture for at least 30 minutes. Rinse under cold water to remove the 2 teaspoons (12 g) of the salt and then pat dry thoroughly using paper towels. Chop the eggplant into bite-sized cubes and set aside.

2. Add the olive oil to the Instant Pot. Press "Sauté" and wait a minute or two for the olive oil to get hot. Add the onion and sauté for 2 to 3 minutes. Then add in the garlic and stir for 30 seconds. And in the cubed eggplant and cook for 3 minutes, stirring frequently.

3. Pour the water in and stir. Press the "Cancel" button to exit the sauté mode. Pour the crushed tomatoes, tomato sauce, rotini, sugar, Italian seasoning, chili flakes, ½ teaspoon of the salt and pepper on top. DO NOT STIR.

4. Secure the lid and press the "Pressure Cook" button until the display light is under "HIGH" and use the "-/+" button to adjust the time to 6 minutes. Be sure the valve on top is set to sealing. Once the pasta is done, quick release the pressure and once the pin drops, remove the lid. Give the pasta a good stir.

5. Taste and adjust the seasonings. Garnish with Parmesan cheese and fresh basil.

TAWNIE'S TIP: Sweating the eggplant (Step 1) is helpful for this recipe to prevent the eggplant from getting soggy. I tested without sweating it, and it wasn't as yummy!

EASY PEASY FETTUCCINE ALFREDO

YIELD: 4–6 SERVINGS
TOTAL TIME: 30 MINUTES

3 cups (720 ml) vegetable broth

1 lb (454 g) fettuccine noodles, uncooked

½ cup (112 g) unsalted butter, divided

1 tsp garlic, minced

1 tsp kosher salt

½ tsp Italian seasoning

½ tsp white pepper

Pinch of fresh nutmeg

1 cup (240 ml) heavy cream

1 cup (100 g) Parmigiano-Reggiano cheese, finely grated

Garnish

Black pepper

Parmesan cheese

Flat leaf Italian parsley

When I was about 10 years old, I claimed I didn't like red sauce and persisted in ordering Alfredo pasta only. My Italian father shook his head and never understood but continued to order my fettuccine Alfredo for me. I am obsessed with anything marinara or red sauce now (phew!) but equally still have a place in my heart for creamy, cheesy white sauces too. It doesn't take much to make an insanely delicious fettuccine Alfredo and the Instant Pot makes it extremely easy. While the ingredient list is simple, this meal turns out to be an impressively elegant and rich pasta loaded with flavors of Parmigiano-Reggiano cheese and perfectly cooked, intensely creamy al dente noodles that I know you'll love.

1. Pour the vegetable broth into the pot. Break the fettuccine noodles in half and sprinkle them in a random, crisscross pattern. This helps prevent the noodles from sticking together. Add 4 tablespoons (57 g) of butter and the garlic on top. Gently press the noodles down, DO NOT STIR, so they're covered mostly by the broth.

2. Secure the lid. Press the "Pressure Cook" button until the display light is under "HIGH" and use the "-/+" button to adjust the time to 7 minutes. Be sure the valve on top is set to sealing. Once the timer sounds, allow the pressure to naturally release for 5 minutes. Quick release the remaining steam.

3. Once the pin drops, remove the lid and stir the pasta to break up any noodles that may have stuck together. Stir in the remaining 4 tablespoons (57 g) of butter, salt, Italian seasoning, white pepper and nutmeg. Lastly, add in the heavy cream and Parmigiano-Reggiano cheese and stir until the noodles are coated.

4. Taste and adjust the seasonings, as desired. If the sauce doesn't seem thick enough, allow the noodles to rest and the sauce will come together. Serve with freshly grated pepper, more Parmesan cheese and fresh parsley.

TAWNIE'S TIP: The thing about Alfredo is the sauce will thicken as the pasta sits. To easily loosen the sauce up, heat in a skillet over medium heat and add in a little more heavy cream to make it creamy again.

3 CHEESE ITALIAN MAC AND CHEESE

YIELD: 8 SERVINGS

TOTAL TIME: 30 MINUTES

For the macaroni

1 lb (454 g) medium shells

3½ cups (840 ml) water

1 cup (180 g) petite diced tomatoes

4 tbsp (56 g) unsalted butter

2 tsp Italian seasoning

1 tsp garlic powder

1 tsp kosher salt

1 cup (108 g) shredded fontina cheese

1 cup (100 g) shredded Parmesan cheese

1 cup (113 g) shredded provolone cheese

12 oz (354 ml) evaporated milk

2 tsp (5 g) cornstarch

½ cup (10 g) fresh basil, chopped

Salt and pepper, to taste

For the breadcrumb topping

1 tbsp (15 ml) olive oil

1 cup (56 g) Panko breadcrumbs

4 cloves garlic, minced

¼ cup (25 g) shredded Parmesan cheese

¼ cup (15 g) chopped fresh flat leaf Italian parsley

If you haven't noticed yet by this point in the book, pasta and cheese is my love language. This three cheese Italian style macaroni and cheese is ultra-creamy and making it in the Instant Pot is a breeze. And trust me, the Panko Parmesan breadcrumbs are worth the extra step of using the stove!

1. Add the shells, water, diced tomatoes, butter, Italian seasoning, garlic powder and salt into the Instant Pot and DO NOT STIR.

2. Secure the lid in place with the steam vent sealed. Press the "Pressure Cook" button until the display light is under "HIGH" and use the "-/+" button to adjust the time until the display reads 5 minutes.

3. While the pasta cooks, make the breadcrumb topping. In a small frying pan over medium heat, add the olive oil. When hot, add the Panko breadcrumbs and the garlic. Cook until golden, for 3 minutes. Be sure to keep an eye on them and stir occasionally to prevent burning. Remove from heat and stir in the Parmesan cheese and parsley. Set the breadcrumbs aside in a bowl.

4. Once the timer sounds, quick release the pressure. When the pin drops, remove the lid.

5. Press "Cancel" and then select the "Sauté" button. Stir the pasta to combine. Then gradually stir in small handfuls of the cheeses, allowing it to melt in between additions, until all the cheeses are added.

6. Whisk together the evaporated milk and cornstarch and stir into the pasta. Add in the fresh basil. Taste the pasta and add salt and pepper as desired.

7. Serve with the toasted breadcrumbs on top and enjoy!

TAWNIE'S TIPS:

- You can use the entire can of diced tomatoes if you prefer more tomatoes.
- Take a little extra time to grate the cheese yourself instead of buying pre-shredded cheese. This goes for all my recipes, but it is particularly important to create the best texture for this mac and cheese recipe.

PASTA PUTTANESCA

YIELD: 2–4 SERVINGS
TOTAL TIME: 25 MINUTES

2 cups (480 ml) water

8 oz (227 g) spaghetti, uncooked

2 tbsp (30 ml) olive oil

1 tsp kosher salt

24 oz (680 g) jarred marinara sauce

⅓ cup (60 g) chopped kalamata olives

⅓ cup (40 g) capers

½ tsp dried oregano

Pinch of red pepper chili flakes

¼ cup (25 g) finely grated Parmesan cheese

¼ cup (10 g) fresh basil, chopped

¼ cup (15 g) chopped fresh flat leaf Italian parsley

Garnish

Lemon zest

Parmesan cheese (optional)

This pasta is bursting with flavor thanks to the briny capers, rich tomato base and salty olives. Since this is a meatless main, I've opted to omit the anchovy filets, but feel free to add them if you'd like a more traditional puttanesca sauce. This is a delicious recipe to break up the normal routine and I've said it before, but I'll say it again—it's really easy to make! I know you'll devour this flavor-packed Italian classic!

1. Pour the water into the pot. Break the spaghetti noodles in half and sprinkle them in a random, crisscross pattern. This helps prevent the noodles from sticking together. Add the olive oil and salt on top. DO NOT STIR.

2. Add in the marinara, olives, capers, oregano and chili flakes. Once again, do not stir.

3. Secure the lid in place with the steam vent sealed. Press the "Pressure Cook" button until the display light is under "HIGH" and use the "-/+" button to adjust the time until the display reads 8 minutes.

4. Once the timer sounds, quick release the pressure. When the pin drops, remove the lid. Stir the pasta. Then add in the Parmesan, basil and parsley and stir until combined.

5. Serve with a dusting of lemon zest on top and additional Parmesan cheese, if desired.

TAWNIE'S TIP: To clean the small nooks and crannies of your Instant Pot, try using a small foam paintbrush to get in those hard to reach spots!

ROSÉ RIGATONI

YIELD: 6–8 SERVINGS
TOTAL TIME: 30 MINUTES

1 lb (454 g) rigatoni, uncooked

3 cups (720 ml) vegetable broth or water

16.9 oz (479 g) jarred Alfredo sauce

24 oz (680 g) jarred marinara sauce

1 tsp onion powder

1 tsp garlic powder

1 tsp dried basil

1 tsp Italian seasoning

1 tsp kosher salt

¼ tsp pepper

4 oz (116 g) softened cream cheese

¼ cup (25 g) finely grated Parmesan cheese

Garnish

Fresh basil

Parmesan cheese

This luxuriously creamy tomato-based sauce (rosé sauce) is made with Alfredo sauce to give it a gorgeous light pink color. It is one of my favorite pastas for an easy date night in dinner, and it only takes 30 minutes to bring together. It's absolutely delicious, full of flavor and one of the easiest pasta recipes in this book!

1. Add the rigatoni to the bottom of the Instant Pot. Pour the vegetable broth on top of the pasta. DO NOT STIR, but gently press the noodles down so they are mostly covered by the broth. They won't entirely be submerged and that is okay.

2. Add the Alfredo sauce, then the marinara sauce and then the onion powder, garlic powder, dried basil, Italian seasoning, salt and pepper on top. Once again, DO NOT STIR.

3. Secure the lid. Press the "Pressure Cook" button until the display light is under "HIGH" and use the "-/+" button to adjust the time to 6 minutes. Be sure the valve on top is set to sealing.

4. Once the timer sounds, allow the pressure to naturally release for 3 minutes. Quick release the remaining steam. Once the pin drops, remove the lid and give the pasta a stir. Add in the cream cheese and Parmesan cheese and stir until incorporated. Garnish with fresh basil and more Parmesan cheese, serve immediately and enjoy!

TAWNIE'S TIP: You can easily serve with chicken, shrimp or stir in cooked ground beef/turkey/sausage for a more substantial meal.

SPINACH AND MUSHROOM MANICOTTI

YIELD: 4-5 SERVINGS
TOTAL TIME: 45 MINUTES

Stuffed manicotti is really fun to make (yes, pasta becomes fun to make once you hit your 30s) and you can feel free to spruce it up with different herbs and seasonings. I chose fresh basil and parsley and kept things simple with garlic powder and onion powder. The manicotti tubes cook beautifully in the Instant Pot and with my method—they don't become flimsy or overcooked.

For the filling

1 cup (112 g) low-moisture mozzarella cheese, divided

¾ cup (185 g) whole milk ricotta

¾ cup (75 g) finely grated Parmesan cheese

6 oz (171 g) frozen spinach, thawed and squeezed

½ cup (130 g) mushrooms, finely chopped

1 large egg

¼ cup (15 g) chopped fresh flat leaf Italian parsley

¼ cup (10 g) chopped fresh basil

1 tsp Italian seasoning

½ tsp garlic powder

½ tsp onion powder

1 tsp kosher salt

½ tsp black pepper

To cook the manicotti

10 manicotti shells (6.4 oz) uncooked

1½ cups (360 ml) vegetable broth

24 oz (680 g) marinara sauce

Garnish

Parmesan cheese

Flat leaf Italian parsley

1. In a large bowl, mix ¾ cup (84 g) mozzarella cheese, whole milk ricotta, Parmesan cheese, frozen spinach, mushrooms, egg, parsley, basil, Italian seasoning, garlic powder, onion powder, salt and pepper to make the filling.

2. Stuff the spinach-mushroom-cheese mixture into the manicotti using a piping bag or squeeze the cheese filling into a plastic baggie and cut the corner off to use as a makeshift piping bag.

3. Pour the vegetable broth into the Instant Pot and select "Sauté." Bring the broth to a simmer, which takes 4 to 5 minutes, and then press "Cancel."

4. Carefully set the trivet down into the pot on top of the broth. Place 5 manicotti on top of the trivet in a single layer and spoon some of the marinara sauce over them. Then place the remaining 5 manicotti on top and cover with marinara sauce. Be sure the manicotti noodles are covered completely by the sauce.

5. Press the "Pressure Cook" button until the display light is under "HIGH" and use the "-/+" button to adjust the time to 6 minutes. Be sure the valve on top is set to sealing. Once the manicotti is done, allow the pressure to naturally release for 5 minutes. Then release any of the remaining pressure.

6. Remove the lid, sprinkle the remaining ¼ cup (28 g) mozzarella cheese on top and replace the lid to melt the cheese. Serve with more marinara, as desired. Garnish with Parmesan cheese and chopped flat leaf Italian parsley.

TAWNIE'S TIPS:

- Use a food processor to chop the mushrooms into a fine texture. It's the perfect hack to spend less time chopping!

- If you find the manicotti is still too al dente, replace the lid to allow the residual steam to finish cooking the noodles.

CRAZY GOOD CACIO E PEPE

YIELD: 4 SERVINGS
TOTAL TIME: 20 MINUTES

4 cups (960 ml) vegetable broth, or water

1 lb (454 g) spaghetti, uncooked, broken in half

4 tbsp (56 g) unsalted butter

2 tsp (4 g) peppercorns

2 tbsp (30 ml) olive oil

2 cups (170 g) finely grated Pecorino Romano

½ tsp kosher salt, plus more to taste

This dish features a creamy, Pecorino Romano–spiked sauce that gloriously coats each spirally spaghetti noodle stand. It's quite simple, especially when reviewing the ingredient list, but it is truly indulgent and packs in tons of flavor. It's basically really good pasta with cheese and pepper and there's not a more effortless combination that's made me happier. I'm filing this one under meatless mains, but it works as a praiseworthy pasta and also even a side too . . . I just want to eat it as a snack all day 24/7.

1. Pour the vegetable broth into the Instant Pot. Add the uncooked spaghetti on top in a crisscross pattern and gently press down into the broth, but DO NOT STIR. Add the butter on top.

2. Secure the lid and press the "Pressure Cook" button until the display light is under "HIGH" and use the "-/+" button to adjust the time to 8 minutes. Be sure the valve on top is set to sealing.

3. Meanwhile, crush the peppercorns using a mortar and pestle and add them to a small skillet over medium heat with the olive oil. Once fragrant, after 1 minute, remove from the heat.

4. Once the pasta is done, quick release the steam. When the pin drops, remove the lid. Stir the pasta to combine. The cheese and pasta will absorb the broth so no need to drain it.

5. Add the Pecorino Romano, toasted peppercorn olive oil and the salt. Stir to combine. Taste and adjust any seasonings as needed (mainly more pepper or cheese) and enjoy!

TAWNIE'S TIP: Be sure to use Pecorino Romano and not Parmesan. Pecorino Romano is much more flavorful and important to this specific pasta.

PAPPARDELLE AL PESTO

YIELD: 4 SERVINGS
TOTAL TIME: 15 MINUTES

8 oz (227 g) pappardelle pasta, uncooked

4 cups (960 ml) filtered water

½ cup (133 g) Everyday Pesto (page 144)

¼ cup (60 ml) reserved pasta water

Garnish

Fresh basil

Parmesan cheese

This recipe uses my favorite Everyday Pesto recipe (page 144) and tosses it together with big, bouncy pappardelle pasta. Pesto comes from the Italian word, "pestare," which translates to "to grind or crush," which is why I use a mortar and pestle when I make homemade pesto. Nowadays, many people like to use a food processor to bring the pesto together which is fine too! A homemade pesto looks more rustic than a store-bought one and a little goes a long way to dress up the pasta. It's all about using quality ingredients to make the most out of simple meals like this one.

1. Add the pappardelle into the Instant Pot and pour the water over the pasta. DO NOT STIR, but if needed, press the noodles down gently to make sure most of the pasta is covered by water.

2. Secure the lid and press the "Pressure Cook" button until the display light is under "HIGH" and use the "-/+" button to adjust the time to 3 minutes. Be sure the valve on top is set to sealing.

3. Meanwhile, make the homemade pesto according to the recipe on page 144.

4. Perform a "controlled quick release" which means press on the steam release valve for about 5 seconds and then stop for a couple seconds. Repeat this until all the pressure has been released. If you don't release the pressure this way, the valve will spit out a lot of water and it can get messy.

5. Reserve ¼ cup (60 ml) of the pasta water and drain the rest. Add the cooked pasta back into the pot and stir in the pesto. Add 1 tablespoon (15 ml) of the pasta water at a time until desired consistency is reached. Garnish the pasta with fresh basil and freshly grated Parmesan cheese. Enjoy!

TAWNIE'S TIP: A great tip for cooking pasta in the Instant Pot is to take the amount of time the pasta package says it takes to cook and divide whatever the lowest number is by 2 and then subtract 1 from that number. Whatever you arrive at is typically how long to cook on HIGH pressure in the Instant Pot.

QUICK AND EASY BRUSCHETTA PASTA

YIELD: 4 SERVINGS
TOTAL TIME: 20 MINUTES

8 oz (226 g) farfalle pasta, uncooked

2 cups (480 ml) water

¼ cup (60 ml) aged balsamic vinegar

1 oz fresh basil, chopped

2 tbsp (30 ml) olive oil

5 cloves garlic, finely grated or pressed

1 tbsp (15 ml) lemon juice, freshly squeezed

½ tsp kosher salt

¼ tsp black pepper

Pinch of red pepper chili flakes

1 cup (140 g) cherry tomatoes, halved

1 cup (225 g) fresh mozzarella balls

¼ cup (25 g) finely grated Parmesan cheese

Garnish

Balsamic reduction

Fresh basil

Parmesan cheese

Say hello to your favorite appetizer turned into a light, refreshing, 20-minute pasta. You'll love the pop of color from the garden-fresh cherry tomatoes contrasting with the vibrant green basil in this nice and light meal. It's filled with a tangy balsamic reduction and creamy mozzarella cheese balls, and the farfalle pasta act like little shovels scooping up all the yummy goodness in each bite. It's truly quick and easy and I love serving it both warm and cold!

1. Add the farfalle to the bottom of the Instant Pot. Pour the water on top of the pasta. DO NOT STIR, but gently press the noodles down so they are mostly covered by the water. They won't entirely be submerged and that is okay.

2. Secure the lid in place with the steam vent sealed. Press the "Pressure Cook" button and use the "-/+" button to adjust the time until the display reads 5 minutes.

3. Meanwhile in a small mixing bowl, combine the balsamic vinegar, basil, olive oil, garlic, lemon juice, salt, pepper and chili flakes. Set this aside.

4. Once the timer sounds, quick release the steam. Once the pin drops, remove the lid. Then, drain and rinse the pasta and then add it back to the Instant Pot. Add in the balsamic mixture. Then, stir in the cherry tomatoes, mozzarella and Parmesan cheese. Taste and adjust seasonings as desired.

5. Serve with a generous drizzle of balsamic reduction on top, basil and Parmesan cheese. I love this pasta either warm or cold!

TAWNIE'S TIPS:

- My family and I love to enjoy this with grilled chicken, shrimp, or salmon for a lean protein option.

- I typically use store-bought balsamic reduction for ease, but if you want to make your own it's also really easy to make. In a saucepan over medium heat, combine 1 cup (240 ml) balsamic vinegar and ¼ cup (50 g) brown sugar until the sugar dissolves. Reduce to a simmer for 15 to 20 minutes or until the glaze reduces and can coat the back of a spoon.

ORZO AND VEGETABLE STUFFED PEPPERS

YIELD: 4 SERVINGS

TOTAL TIME: 35 MINUTES

4 medium, colorful bell peppers (I love red, green and orange)

2 tbsp (30 ml) olive oil

1 small white onion, diced

4 oz (120 g) white mushrooms, chopped

1 small head broccoli, diced small

1 small zucchini, diced small

2 cups (450 g) cooked orzo pasta (1 cup [170 g] uncooked yields about 2 cups cooked)

1 ¼ cup (280 g) marinara sauce, divided

½ cup (50 g) finely grated Parmesan cheese

¼ cup (30 g) Italian breadcrumbs

1 tsp Italian seasoning

1 tsp garlic powder

1 tsp dried parsley

1 tsp dried basil

1 tsp kosher salt

¼ tsp black pepper

1 cup (240 ml) water

½ cup (56 g) mozzarella cheese, shredded

Garnish
Fresh flat leaf Italian parsley

You'll be wanting to put these gorgeous peppers in regular rotation from the first moment you devour them. What I love about stuffed peppers in the Instant Pot is that you can totally skip over the long 1 hour bake time in the oven and you don't have to cook the bell peppers before stuffing them either.

1. Slice the tops off the bell peppers and remove the seeds and membranes. Rinse the bell peppers to remove any stubborn seeds. Set aside.

2. Add the olive oil to the Instant Pot. Press "Sauté" and wait 1 to 2 minutes for the oil to get hot. Add in the onion, mushrooms, broccoli and zucchini. Sauté for 5 to 7 minutes or until the vegetables have softened. Press "Cancel" to exit the sauté function.

3. Add the veggies to a large mixing bowl. Then, stir in the cooked orzo with 1 cup (224 g) marinara sauce, the Parmesan cheese, breadcrumbs, Italian seasoning, garlic powder, dried parsley, dried basil, salt and pepper.

4. Stuff each bell pepper to the brim with the orzo vegetable mixture (you may have a little leftover filling based on the size of your bell peppers). Clean out the Instant Pot and then pour 1 cup (240 ml) water in the bottom. Set the trivet in the pot and stand the bell peppers on the trivet. Spoon about 1 tablespoon (14 g) of marinara sauce on top of each bell pepper.

5. Secure the lid. Press the "Pressure Cook" button until the display light is under "HIGH" and use the "-/+" button to adjust the time to 4 minutes. Be sure the valve on top is set to sealing. Quick release the pressure and once the pin drops, remove the lid. Sprinkle the tops with mozzarella cheese and replace the lid until the residual steam melts the cheese over the bell peppers. Using tongs or a large spoon, gently lift the bell peppers out onto serving plates. Garnish with parsley and enjoy!

TAWNIE'S TIPS:

- Chop up the bell pepper from the tops that were cut off and sauté with the rest of the vegetables for minimal food waste.

- If you find the bell peppers are hard and not cooked enough, replace the lid to allow the residual steam to finish cooking the bell peppers.

Savory Soups

If there is anything that will convince you that an Instant Pot deserves a permanent place on your kitchen counter, it is these soup recipes. Soups are probably my favorite thing to make in the Instant Pot but don't get me wrong . . . I am literally obsessed with making anything I can in it, but soups just top the list. They are soup-er easy to make, soup-er delicious and soup-er nourishing (OKAY, I'LL STOP).

In this chapter you'll find rich and hearty soups like my Sausage Tortellini Soup (page 90) and Loaded Pizza Soup (page 97), and lighter but satisfying soups like my Vegetarian Lentil Soup (page 101) and Sicilian Chicken Noodle Soup (page 93).

These soup recipes come together in a flash, and I am continually amazed at how flavorful each soup is when made in the pressure cooker. Plus, you don't have to crowd the stove with a big soup pot or continuously stir to make sure the bottom doesn't burn. I love that the only task is a little sautéing of vegetables and browning of the meat, pouring the remaining ingredients in, then setting it and forgetting about it until it's done! Dinner can cook while you get a load of laundry started, feed the dogs, or just take a few minutes to relax on the couch!

Just because the Instant Pot is an efficient and effective appliance doesn't mean that these soups skimp on any flavor. In fact, very little moisture escapes when pressure cooking, resulting in a more rich, flavorful and elevated soup. Hello deliciousness!

I hope you love these soup recipes and I am so excited to help you get a cozy, quick and delicious dinner on the table.

ITALIAN SAUSAGE MINESTRONE SOUP

YIELD: 8–10 SERVINGS
TOTAL TIME: 45 MINUTES

2 tbsp (30 ml) olive oil, divided

1 lb (454 g) hot ground Italian sausage

2 large carrots, small dice

3 ribs celery, chopped

1 small yellow onion, diced

5 cloves garlic, pressed

1 tbsp (16 g) tomato paste

1 tbsp (5 g) Italian seasoning

2 tsp (4 g) fennel seed

1 (28-oz [794-g]) can crushed tomatoes

1 (8-oz [227-g]) can tomato sauce

¼ cup (62 g) sun-dried tomato pesto

1 large russet potato washed and peeled, diced into small pieces (about 2 cups [258 g], soaked in water to prevent browning)

1 cup (110 g) fresh green beans, trimmed and cut into 1-inch (2.5-cm) pieces

4 cups (960 ml) vegetable broth (may sub chicken broth)

2 cups (480 ml) water

2 bay leaves

Don't you just love a warm bowl of minestrone? In all my years of blogging and developing recipes, this is my all-time favorite minestrone. And before you say anything, don't let the lengthy ingredient list intimidate you! Most of these ingredients might already be populating your pantry. This super cozy, veggie-packed soup is made with hearty Italian sausage, ditalini pasta and pantry staples like crushed tomatoes and kidney beans. Get ready for leftovers because this recipe makes a big batch. You will have plenty to serve or freeze to enjoy for weeks on end!

1. Add 1 tablespoon (15 ml) of olive oil to the bottom of the Instant Pot. Press "Sauté" and once the oil is hot, add in the Italian sausage. Break up the meat with a wooden spoon until it is no longer pink. Remove the sausage, leaving the little brown bits in the pot and set the meat aside.

2. Add in the remaining olive oil and add in the carrots, celery and onion. Stir occasionally and sauté until fragrant, for 3 to 4 minutes. Add in the garlic and cook for 30 seconds more. Add in the tomato paste and stir to coat the vegetables.

3. Add the sausage back in. Then add in the Italian seasoning, fennel seeds, crushed tomatoes, tomato sauce, sun-dried tomato pesto, diced potato, green beans, broth, water and bay leaves. Stir to combine. Secure the lid and press "Cancel" to exit the sauté mode. Press the "Pressure Cook" button until the display light is under "HIGH" and use the "–/+" button to adjust the time to 3 minutes. Be sure the valve on top is set to sealing.

(continued)

1 cup (168 g) ditalini pasta

1 (15-oz [425-g]) can kidney beans, drained and rinsed

1 (15-oz [425-g]) can great northern beans, drained and rinsed

10 oz (284 g) frozen spinach, thawed and excess water squeezed out

2 tbsp (30 ml) fresh lemon juice

Garnish

Freshly grated Parmesan cheese

Red pepper chili flakes

4. Meanwhile, bring a large pot of salted water to boil over medium-high heat. Cook the ditalini pasta (or any small pasta shape of choice) according to the package directions. Drain and set the pasta aside.

5. Once the timer sounds, let the pot sit undisturbed to allow the pressure to naturally release for 10 minutes. Then, quick release any of the remaining pressure. Once the pin drops, remove the lid.

6. Remove and discard the bay leaves. Add the kidney and great northern beans, spinach and lemon juice. Stir to combine. Spoon some of the cooked pasta into a bowl and ladle the soup on top. Garnish with your favorite soup toppings and enjoy.

TAWNIE'S TIPS:

- Freezer instructions: Allow the soup to cool completely and store in freezer-safe containers for up to 3 months. Thaw soup overnight in the fridge and warm on the stove in a saucepan.

- Make this vegan by omitting the Italian sausage and using a vegan cheese, if desired.

- I tested this recipe by cooking the pasta in the soup, but the pasta was mushy and soaked up all the liquid. I found it best for this recipe to cook the pasta separately and add it into the soup when you are ready to eat.

ITALIAN WEDDING SOUP

YIELD: 6 SERVINGS
TOTAL TIME: 40 MINUTES

For the meatballs

1 slice white bread, cut into ½-inch (1.3-cm) cubes with crust removed

2 tbsp (30 ml) whole milk

1 lb (454 g) ground beef

⅓ cup (33 g) finely grated Parmesan cheese

1 large egg

3 tbsp (12 g) minced fresh flat leaf Italian parsley

2 tbsp (20 g) grated white onion

1 tsp garlic, pressed

1 tsp kosher salt

Cracked black pepper, to taste

For the soup

2 tbsp (30 ml) olive oil

1 medium yellow onion, finely chopped

3 large carrots, peeled and sliced into thin circles

3 ribs celery, thinly sliced

3 cloves garlic, pressed

1 tsp Italian seasoning

1 tsp kosher salt

¼ tsp black pepper

This Italian Wedding Soup makes a nourishing lunch or even a hearty first course. Perfectly seasoned homemade meatballs make any soup better and they put this soup over the top. It's also chock-full of vibrant veggies and lots of acini de pepe pasta all tucked away in a rich and flavorful broth. It is literally the perfect marriage of flavors. And the best part is that nobody has to be getting married to enjoy this lovely union of meatballs, broth and veggies!

1. To make the meatballs, soak the cut bread pieces and the milk for 5 minutes in a large bowl. Add in the ground beef, Parmesan cheese, egg, parsley, white onion, garlic, salt and pepper. Gently mix with clean hands or a spoon until just combined.

2. Portion out the meatballs using a 2-tablespoon (15-ml) scoop and gently roll in your hands. Set the meatballs on a parchment paper–lined baking sheet. You should get around 25 small meatballs.

3. Pour the olive oil into the Instant Pot. Press "Sauté" and wait 1 to 2 minutes for the Instant Pot to get hot. Add in the onion, carrots and celery and cook, stirring occasionally, for 3 to 4 minutes. Add in the garlic, Italian seasoning, salt and pepper and stir for 30 seconds.

(continued)

8 cups (1.9 L) chicken stock

½ cup (50 g) acini de pepe pasta, uncooked

5 cups (150 g) fresh baby spinach, roughly chopped

Garnish

Freshly grated Parmesan cheese

4. Add in the chicken stock and then carefully add in the meatballs.

5. Secure the lid in place with the steam vent sealed. Press "Pressure Cook" on "HIGH" pressure and use the "-/+" button to adjust the time until the display reads 4 minutes. When the soup is done, quick release the steam. Once the pin drops, remove the lid.

6. Press "Cancel" and then select the "Sauté" button again. Add in the pasta and cook for 8 minutes. Stir in the spinach and season to taste with more salt and pepper. Garnish with Parmesan cheese and enjoy!

TAWNIE'S TIPS:

- As the soup sits, the pasta will absorb the broth. Thin out the soup with more broth as desired.

- Make the meatballs in advance, cover and place them in the fridge for 1 day until you're ready to make the soup.

- Feel free to cook the pasta in a pot on the stove and add it separately to the soup to avoid the pasta soaking up the broth. This is great if you plan to make this for meal prep and aren't serving the soup immediately.

CREAMY TOMATO WHITE BEAN SOUP WITH PESTO

YIELD: 6–8 SERVINGS
TOTAL TIME: 45 MINUTES

For the soup

3 tbsp (42 g) unsalted butter

1 medium yellow onion, diced

2 large carrots, diced

2 tsp (12 g) kosher salt, divided

1 tbsp (9 g) garlic, pressed

3 cups (720 ml) chicken broth

1 (15-oz [425-ml]) can cannellini beans, drained and rinsed

2 (14-oz [396-g]) cans crushed tomatoes

2 tbsp (30 g) granulated sugar

½ cup (120 ml) heavy cream

For the pesto

1 recipe Everyday Pesto (page 144)

Garnish

Pesto, of course!

Freshly grated Parmesan cheese

Freshly ground black pepper

A few neglected cans of white beans and crushed tomatoes and a scoop of leftover pesto were the inspiration for this amazing recipe. It's such a simple soup, but the vivid contrasts of color, textures and flavors make it work. Sure, tomato soup is incredible on its own, but the pesto especially welcomes bright, aromatic and herby flavors and against the creamy tomato soup, the basil pesto gleams. The white beans give the broth body, and I know you'll love the tasty twist I've put on this old favorite.

1. Press "Sauté" and add the butter to the Instant Pot. Once the butter melts, add the onion and carrots. Cook, stirring frequently, for 5 minutes or until the onion has softened. Mix in 1 teaspoon of salt and the garlic. Stir for 30 seconds.

2. Press "Cancel" to exit the sauté mode and then add in the chicken broth, beans, crushed tomatoes and sugar. Stir to combine.

3. Secure the lid in place. Press the "Pressure Cook" button until the display light is under "HIGH" and use the "-/+" button to adjust the time to 3 minutes. Be sure the valve on top is set to sealing.

4. Meanwhile, make the pesto according to the recipe instructions on page 144.

5. Once the timer sounds, let the pot sit undisturbed to allow the pressure to naturally release for 10 minutes. Then release any of the remaining pressure. Once the pin drops, remove the lid.

6. Stir in the heavy cream. Carefully transfer the soup to a high-powered blender and blend until smooth. (You may need to do this in 2 to 3 batches.) Alternatively, you can use an immersion blender. Serve the soup immediately with pesto on top, freshly grated Parmesan cheese and freshly ground pepper.

TAWNIE'S TIP: Using a mortar and pestle creates an incredible pesto for this soup, but I realize not everyone owns one. Using a food processor to combine the pesto ingredients will also work.

SAUSAGE TORTELLINI SOUP

YIELD: 8 SERVINGS

TOTAL TIME: 40 MINUTES

2 tbsp (30 ml) olive oil

1 lb (454 g) hot ground Italian sausage

1 medium yellow onion, diced

1 medium red bell pepper, diced

2 large carrots, diced

4 ribs celery, diced

3 cloves garlic, pressed

2 tsp Italian seasoning

1 tsp kosher salt

1 tsp brown sugar

¼ tsp black pepper

1 (28-oz [794-g]) can crushed tomatoes

4 cups (960 ml) beef broth

9 oz (255 g) refrigerated three cheese tortellini

4 cups (120 g) fresh baby spinach, roughly chopped

½ cup (120 ml) heavy cream

Garnish

Freshly grated Parmesan cheese

TAWNIE'S TIPS:

- You can use kale instead of spinach if you prefer it.
- I love cheese tortellini but feel free to use your favorite meat tortellini.

You know the saying "hug in a bowl?" This soup is that and more. Cheesy tortellini, Italian sausage, fresh spinach and lots of veggies are all enveloped in a creamy, rich tomato broth. I just adore how fast this soup comes together and how much flavor it packs in! Like most recipes in this book, serving this soup with a mountain of freshly grated Parmesan cheese on top is non-negotiable. I'm telling you . . . if there is one recipe you make from this book, please make this one—but I actually hope you make them all! Grab a cozy sweater and a big bowl of this soup and dig in.

1. Add the olive oil to the Instant Pot. Press "Sauté" and wait 1 to 2 minutes for the Instant Pot to get hot. Add in the Italian sausage and cook, breaking it up with a wooden spoon, for 3 to 4 minutes.

2. Add in the onion, bell pepper, carrots and celery. Once the onion starts to become fragrant and translucent, in 3 to 5 minutes, add in the garlic, Italian seasoning, salt, brown sugar and pepper. Stir to combine. Press "Cancel." Mix in the crushed tomatoes and beef broth.

3. Secure the lid with the vent in the sealing position. Press "Pressure Cook" until the display light is underneath "HIGH." Use the "-/+" button to adjust the time until the display reads 5 minutes.

4. Once the timer sounds, let the pot sit undisturbed to allow the pressure to naturally release for 5 minutes. Then, quick release any of the remaining pressure.

5. Once the pin drops, remove the lid and press the "Sauté" button again. Stir in the tortellini and the spinach. Allow the soup to come to a boil, stirring occasionally. The tortellini will float to the top once they are cooked in 4 to 5 minutes. Lastly add in the heavy cream and stir. Taste and add in more salt or pepper, as desired.

6. Ladle the soup into bowls and enjoy with freshly grated Parmesan cheese on top.

SICILIAN CHICKEN NOODLE SOUP

YIELD: 6 SERVINGS
TOTAL TIME: 45 MINUTES

2 tbsp (28 g) unsalted butter

1 medium yellow onion, diced

3 large skinny carrots, peeled and thinly sliced

4 ribs celery, thinly sliced

1 small red bell pepper, seeded and diced small

1 tsp kosher salt , plus more to taste

1 tsp garlic, pressed

7 cups (1.7 L) chicken stock

1 (14.5-oz [411-g]) can diced tomatoes with basil, garlic and oregano

¼ cup (15 g) chopped fresh flat leaf Italian parsley

1 bay leaf

1 lb (454 g) raw chicken breasts, boneless, skinless (approximately 2 breasts)

¾ cup (75 g) ditalini pasta, uncooked

1 tbsp (15 ml) freshly squeezed lemon juice

Garnish

Chopped parsley

Freshly grated Parmesan cheese

Crusty bread, for serving

There are so many varieties of chicken noodle soup, but *this* Italian chicken noodle soup in particular is captivating. The classic combination of tender vegetables, flavorful broth and juicy chicken pieces add irresistible cozy vibes and fill you with comfort. This soup can certainly stand alone as a meal, but with crusty bread getting dunked and mingling in with broth and veggies, it's even more hearty. Pass this sensational soup recipe on to anyone who needs a flu-fighting meal or just something to warm the soul on a cold day.

1. Press "Sauté" and add the butter to the Instant Pot. Once the butter melts, add the onion, carrots, celery and bell pepper. Cook, stirring frequently, for 5 minutes or until vegetables have softened. Stir in the salt and the garlic for 30 seconds.

2. Press "Cancel" to turn off the sauté mode. Add in the chicken stock, diced tomatoes, parsley and bay leaf and stir. Nestle the chicken into the broth mixture.

3. Secure the lid in place with the steam vent sealed. Press "Pressure Cook" until the display light is underneath "HIGH" and use the "-/+" button to adjust the time until the display reads 7 minutes. The soup will take about 15 minutes to come to pressure.

4. Once the timer sounds, let the pot sit undisturbed to allow the pressure to naturally release for 10 minutes. Then, release any of the remaining pressure. Once the pin drops, remove the lid.

5. Remove and discard the bay leaf. Remove the chicken and cut into small cubes. Add the chicken back into the soup and stir.

6. Press "Cancel" and then select the "Sauté" button again. Add in the pasta and lemon juice and cook for about 10 minutes, stirring occasionally. Taste the soup and season with additional salt and pepper if desired. Serve immediately with fresh parsley, Parmesan and bread—of course!

TAWNIE'S TIP: Swap the ditalini for pastina pasta or any small pasta shape.

EASY PASTA E FAGIOLI

YIELD: 8 SERVINGS
TOTAL TIME: 35 MINUTES

1 tbsp (15 ml) olive oil

1 lb (454 g) hot ground Italian sausage

1 medium yellow onion, diced

2 large carrots, peeled and sliced into thin circles

3 ribs celery, finely chopped or thinly sliced if you prefer

2 cloves garlic, pressed

4 cups (960 ml) chicken stock

1 (15-oz [425-g]) can tomato sauce

1 (14.5-oz [411-g]) can diced tomatoes with basil and oregano seasonings

1 tbsp (16 g) tomato paste

Pinch of red pepper chili flakes (optional)

2 (15-oz [425-ml]) cans white beans, drained and rinsed

1 cup (100 g) ditalini pasta, uncooked

2 generous cups (134 g) Tuscan kale, roughly chopped, stems removed

Salt and pepper, to taste

Garnish
Freshly grated Parmesan cheese

This classic, comforting soup is a meal in itself, especially with crusty bread for dipping. Perfumed with fresh garlic, basil, oregano and hot Italian sausage, it fills the kitchen with its fragrant Italian aromas. The secret to a delicious soup, in my opinion, is cutting all the vegetables into a small, uniform size. Think about how big you want them to be on your spoon when you take a bite; you want to make it easy to scoop and enjoy this mouth-watering soup by the spoonful!

1. Pour the olive oil into the Instant Pot. Press "Sauté" and wait a minute or two for the Instant Pot to get hot. Add in the Italian sausage and cook, breaking it up with a wooden spoon, for 3 to 4 minutes.

2. Add in the onion, carrots and celery. Stir frequently and cook for another 3 to 4 minutes, or until the vegetables are fragrant. Add in the garlic and stir for 30 seconds.

3. Pour in the chicken stock, tomato sauce, diced tomatoes, tomato paste, chili flakes, if using, white beans and ditalini pasta. Stir everything to combine.

4. Secure the lid in place with the steam vent sealed. Press "Cancel" to exit the sauté mode and then press the "Soup" setting. Use the "-/+" button to adjust the time until the display reads 5 minutes.

5. Once the soup is done, quick release the steam. Once the pin drops, remove the lid.

6. Stir in the chopped kale. Taste and season with salt and pepper, if needed. Ladle the soup into bowls. Garnish with freshly grated Parmesan cheese and enjoy!

TAWNIE'S TIP: Since the pasta noodles are cooked in this soup, they will absorb a lot of the broth as the soup sits. Add more broth when reheating if preferred.

LOADED PIZZA SOUP

YIELD: 6–8 PEOPLE
TOTAL TIME: 45 MINUTES

2 tbsp (30 ml) olive oil

1 lb (454 g) ground beef

½ cup (70 g) mini pepperoni, quartered

8 oz (224 g) white mushrooms, chopped

1 small white onion, diced

1 medium zucchini, chopped

2 medium green bell peppers, diced

3 cloves garlic, minced

1 tbsp (14 g) brown sugar

1 tsp fennel

1 tsp Italian seasoning

¼ tsp red pepper chili flakes

4 cups (960 ml) beef broth

1 (14.5-oz [411-g]) can fire-roasted diced tomatoes

1 (14-oz [397-g]) jar red pizza sauce

Garnish

Black olives

Mozzarella cheese

Parmesan cheese

Basil

Croutons

Mark this recipe down for when you want pizza . . . but in a bowl! This loaded pizza soup boasts many layers of mouthwatering flavors from the ground beef and pepperoni to all your favorite supreme pizza vegetable toppings. This soup is perked up with Italian flavors and all pizza lovers will be drawn to this meal. Pizza lends itself to countless variations so feel free to add your favorite toppings to this soup to make it just how you like it!

1. Pour the olive oil into the Instant Pot. Press "Sauté" and wait 1 to 2 minutes for the Instant Pot to get hot. Add in the ground beef and pepperoni and cook, breaking up the beef with a wooden spoon, for 3 to 4 minutes.

2. Add in the mushrooms, onion, zucchini and bell peppers. Cook, stirring occasionally, for 3 to 4 minutes. Then, add in the garlic, brown sugar, fennel, Italian seasoning and chili flakes. Stir for 30 seconds to combine. Press cancel.

3. Add in the beef broth, diced tomatoes and pizza sauce. Stir to combine.

4. Secure the lid in place with the steam vent sealed. Press the "Pressure Cook" button until the display light is under "HIGH" and use the "-/+" button to adjust the time until the display reads 7 minutes.

5. Once the timer sounds, let the pot sit undisturbed to allow the pressure to naturally release for 15 minutes. Then release any of the remaining pressure.

6. Once the pin drops, remove the lid and stir. Ladle the soup into bowls and garnish with your favorite pizza toppings.

TAWNIE'S TIP: Serve with broiled Texas toast with melted cheese/pepperoni on it. Or top the soup with homemade Parmesan croutons and fresh basil!

CREAMY CHICKEN GNOCCHI SOUP

YIELD: 6 SERVINGS
TOTAL TIME: 45 MINUTES

2 tbsp (28 g) unsalted butter

1 medium yellow onion, diced

3 ribs celery, diced

4 cloves garlic, minced

1 sprig fresh rosemary, chopped

2 bay leaves

1 tsp Italian seasoning

1 tsp kosher salt

½ tsp poultry seasoning

½ tsp black pepper

4 cups (960 ml) chicken broth

2 large carrots, julienned

1 lb (454 g) raw chicken breasts, boneless, skinless (about 2 breasts)

1½ cups (360 ml) heavy cream

1 tbsp (8 g) cornstarch

1 lb (454 g) potato gnocchi, shelf stable

2 cups (60 g) baby spinach, roughly chopped

¾ cup (75 g) finely grated Parmesan cheese

1 tbsp (15 ml) lemon juice

Garnish

Cracked black pepper

Parmesan cheese

Olive oil drizzle

Garlic bread, for serving

In this Creamy Chicken Gnocchi Soup, soft, pillowy gnocchi are cuddled in a creamy broth with plenty of fresh herbs, tender chicken and vibrant baby spinach. It's a wonderful soup to enjoy on a chilly evening and even the fussiest of eaters will clamor for a second bowl. You can't help but adore how the potato gnocchi luxuriates in the creamy, vegetable-filled broth. Get ready to enjoy restaurant quality soup right at home in just 45 minutes!

1. Add the butter to the Instant Pot. Press "Sauté" and wait 1 to 2 minutes for the butter to melt. Add the onion and celery and sauté for 2 to 3 minutes. Add the garlic, rosemary, bay leaves, Italian seasoning, salt, poultry seasoning and pepper and stir for 1 minute. Add in the chicken broth and carrots. Stir. Nestle the chicken breasts down into broth.

2. Press "Cancel." Secure the lid with the vent in the sealing position. Press "Pressure Cook" until the display light is underneath "HIGH." Use the "-/+" button to adjust the time until the display reads 8 minutes.

3. Once the timer sounds, let the pot sit undisturbed to allow the pressure to naturally release for 10 minutes. Then, quick release any of the remaining pressure. Once the pin drops, remove the lid.

4. Using tongs, take the chicken out and then shred with two forks. Press "Sauté" on the "less" setting. Whisk the heavy cream and cornstarch together and whisk into the soup. Carefully add in the gnocchi and cook for 7 minutes or until the gnocchi is done. Lastly add the chicken back in, along with the baby spinach, Parmesan cheese and lemon juice. Stir and allow the spinach to wilt for 1 minute.

5. Garnish with cracked black pepper, Parmesan cheese and olive oil and serve with garlic bread.

TAWNIE'S TIPS:

- This soup is wildly delicious with bacon crumbles on top too!
- If you'd like, you can substitute evaporated milk for the heavy cream.

VEGETARIAN LENTIL SOUP

YIELD: 8 SERVINGS
TOTAL TIME: 45 MINUTES

2 tbsp (30 ml) olive oil

1 medium yellow onion

2 large carrots peeled and diced small

4 ribs celery, chopped

1 tsp kosher salt

¼ tsp cracked black pepper, plus more for topping

3 cloves garlic, pressed

1½ cups (280 g) green lentils, rinsed and sorted

1 tsp fresh thyme

1 tsp Italian seasoning

2 bay leaves

⅛ tsp paprika

Pinch of red pepper chili flakes

1 large russet potato, peeled and cubed

4 cups (960 ml) vegetable broth

1 cup (240 ml) filtered water

1 (14.5-oz [411-g]) can fire-roasted diced tomatoes

2 tbsp (30 ml) lemon juice, freshly squeezed

1 tbsp (15 g) sugar

4 cups (120 g) baby spinach, roughly chopped

If you've wished for a staple, cold weather soup as nourishing as it is appealing, your wish has come true. Just one steamy bowl of this wholesome and delicious soup takes the frost out of winter weather. The enticing aroma wafting from your Instant Pot will convince friends and family that you've been cooking this soup all day long, but we all know this stellar recipe took you less than an hour. Meat free and mouthwatering, lentils bring an economical plant protein to this exceedingly flavorful soup.

1. Pour the olive oil into the Instant Pot. Press "Sauté" and wait 1 to 2 minutes for the Instant Pot to get hot. Add in the onion, carrots and celery and cook, stirring occasionally, for 3 to 4 minutes. Add in the salt, pepper and garlic. Stir for 30 seconds to combine.

2. Pour in the green lentils, thyme, Italian seasoning, bay leaves, paprika and chili flakes. Stir. Then, add in the potato, broth, water and tomatoes. Stir and then press "Cancel."

3. Secure the lid in place with the steam vent sealed. Press the "Pressure Cook" button until the display light is under "HIGH" and use the "-/+" button to adjust the time until the display reads 15 minutes.

4. Once the timer sounds, let the pot sit undisturbed to allow the pressure to naturally release for 15 minutes. Then release any of the remaining pressure.

5. Once the pin drops, remove the lid and add in the lemon juice, sugar and baby spinach. Stir until the spinach is wilted. Remove the bay leaves, ladle the soup into bowls and top with cracked black pepper, if desired.

TAWNIE'S TIPS:

- I recommend using green or brown lentils since they hold their shape much better in this soup.

- Be sure to use russet potatoes because their starchy flesh breaks down to thicken the soup.

TUSCAN RAVIOLI SOUP

YIELD: 6-8 SERVINGS
TOTAL TIME: 45 MINUTES

2 tbsp (28 g) unsalted butter

2 tbsp (30 g) olive oil, plus more as needed

6 strips thick-cut bacon, chopped

1 lb (454 g) ground hot Italian sausage

½ bulb fennel, chopped

2 large carrots, diced small

3 cloves garlic, minced

4 cups (960 ml) chicken broth

2 cups (480 ml) filtered water

1 (15-oz [425-g]) can tomato sauce

¼ cup (10 g) fresh basil, chopped

2 tsp (2 g) fresh oregano, chopped

2 bay leaves

4.4 oz (120 g) oil-packed sun-dried tomatoes in Italian herbs, oil drained

5 cups (335 g) Tuscan kale, stems removed, roughly chopped

12 oz (340 g) refrigerated four cheese ravioli, uncooked

Salt and pepper, to taste

⅓ cup (80 ml) heavy cream

Garnish

Freshly grated Parmesan cheese

This is a hearty, filling, stick-to-your-ribs kind of soup. It's a cold weather warmer loaded with bacon, Italian sausage, lots of veggies, fresh herbs and four cheese ravioli. You won't be able to stop enjoying cozy spoonfuls of this deliciousness. Get ready to serve this one up all soup season long!

1. Choose the "Sauté" mode. Add the butter and olive oil and once hot, add the bacon and cook until fully rendered, 8 to 10 minutes. Be sure to stir the bacon frequently so it doesn't stick. If it does, deglaze the bottom with a small splash of water to stir up the brown bits. Remove the bacon to a paper towel–lined plate and set aside. Add the sausage and cook until no longer pink, adding any additional olive oil if necessary. Remove the sausage to a bowl.

2. Add the fennel and carrots and sauté for 5 to 6 minutes, once again adding more olive oil as necessary. Add in the garlic and cook for 30 seconds. Pour in the chicken broth, water and tomato sauce. Add the basil, oregano, bay leaves and sun-dried tomatoes on top. Add the bacon and the sausage back in. DO NOT STIR.

3. Press "Cancel" to exit the sauté mode. Secure the lid with the vent in the sealing position. Press "Pressure Cook" until the display light is underneath "HIGH." Use the "-/+" button to adjust the time until the display reads 3 minutes.

4. When the soup is done, quick release the steam. Once the pin drops, remove the lid. Give the soup a big stir. Remove the bay leaves and discard them. Switch back to the sauté mode. Stir in the kale and add in the ravioli. Cook until the ravioli float to the top. Taste and adjust with more salt or pepper.

5. Lastly, stir in the heavy cream. Ladle the soup into bowls and garnish with Parmesan cheese on top.

TAWNIE'S TIPS:

- Soup with pastas in them don't typically store well since the pasta absorbs most of the broth. If you plan to have leftovers, I recommend cooking the ravioli separately and stirring them in when you're ready to enjoy a bowl.

- Tortellini can be used in place of ravioli.

HERBY WHITE BEAN SOUP

YIELD: 8 SERVINGS
TOTAL TIME: 45 MINUTES

1 tbsp olive oil

1 small white onion, diced

2 large carrots, cut into coins

3 ribs celery, chopped

3 cloves garlic, minced

4 cups (960 ml) chicken or vegetable broth

3 (15.5-oz [440-g]) cans white beans, drained

1 russet potato, peeled and cut into cubes

2 bay leaves

1 sprig fresh rosemary, chopped

1 tsp fresh thyme, chopped

1 tsp fresh oregano, chopped

1 tsp kosher salt

¼ tsp black pepper

¼ tsp red pepper chili flakes

For the parsley dressing

⅓ cup (22 g) finely chopped fresh flat leaf Italian parsley

2 tbsp (30 ml) olive oil

1 tbsp (15 ml) lemon juice

2 cloves (2 tsp) garlic, finely grated

Pinch of salt

Creamy white beans and fresh parsley dressing dance together in a flavorful partnership in this budget-friendly soup. The humble white bean is the perfect base for a cozy, yet light soup and the herby dressing instantly brightens up the entire meal. It's filled with plenty of fresh, aromatic herbs, veggies and is a delightful meatless meal. Once cold weather strikes, soup tends to find a permanent spot in our dinner rotation and this one never disappoints.

1. Add the olive oil to the Instant Pot. Press "Sauté" and wait 1 to 2 minutes for the Instant Pot to get hot. Add in the onion, carrots and celery. Sauté the veggies until they are fragrant and tender, for 4 to 5 minutes. Add in the minced garlic and sauté for 30 seconds.

2. Pour in the chicken broth, beans and potatoes along with the bay leaves, rosemary, thyme, oregano, salt, pepper and chili flakes. Gently stir. Press "Cancel" to exit the sauté mode. Secure the lid with the vent in the sealing position. Press "Pressure Cook" until the display light is underneath "HIGH." Use the "-/+" button to adjust the time until the display reads 6 minutes. The Instant Pot will take about 10 minutes to build to pressure.

3. Meanwhile, make the parsley dressing by combining the parsley, olive oil, lemon juice, garlic and a pinch of salt in a small bowl. Set this aside.

4. Once the timer sounds, let the pot sit undisturbed to allow the pressure to naturally release for 10 minutes. Then, quick release any of the remaining pressure. Once the pin drops, remove the lid. Remove the bay leaves and discard.

5. Carefully ladle 2 to 3 cups of the soup into a high-powered blender and blend until smooth. Pour back into the soup and stir (this helps create a creamy texture for the soup). Taste and adjust the flavor with more salt and pepper.

6. Ladle the soup into bowls and drizzle the parsley dressing over the soup. Serve with crusty bread.

TAWNIE'S TIP: Did you know your Instant Pot comes with a built-in lid holder? The handles on the Instant Pot have holes in them designed to stick the lid in to hold it in place!

Starters and Sides

These starters and sides are some of my absolute favorite recipes and like I've said before, I had so much fun making these recipes for you! Here you will find fresh and tasty meatless appetizers and sides, but I've also got hearty and satisfying options too.

You can cook just about anything in your Instant Pot and it actually does an extraordinary job at steaming vegetables. They retain their nutrients, the cooking time is minimal and of course there is less "babysitting" involved. You'll see for yourself when you make an entire head of cauliflower that is tender and flavor-packed (page 125) and the best Bacon and Parmesan Green Beans you've ever had (page 126).

Another cool thing about the Instant Pot is its ability to cook dried beans with no presoaking required. I made the most tender, white beans in under an hour and turned them into a creamy white bean dip that you'll want to dive into (page 117). It's herby, creamy and super simple to make. You can't go wrong with this dip with crusty bread, veggies or even spreading onto a sandwich.

I could go on and on about how obsessed I am with the Instant Pot and all its abilities but here's the thing . . . I wrote this book all about it so is there really any explanation that needs to be said?! I hope you are equally obsessed and fall in love with the recipes in this chapter. The last thing I'll say is that you MUST make the Homemade Ricotta on page 130. It is truly a game changer and you can find me at the counter eating it with a spoon.

SUN-DRIED TOMATO AND SPINACH ORZO

YIELD: 6 SERVINGS
TOTAL TIME: 20 MINUTES

2 tbsp (28 g) unsalted butter

1 shallot, minced

½ tsp kosher salt

5 cloves garlic, pressed

½ tsp red pepper chili flakes

1 tsp lemon zest

1½ cups (260 g) orzo, uncooked

½ cup (27 g) oil-packed sun-dried tomatoes, oil drained

2¾ cups (660 ml) chicken broth

3 cups (90 g) roughly chopped baby spinach

2 tbsp (5 g) fresh basil chiffonade (see Tip)

1½ cups (150 g) freshly grated Parmesan cheese

2 tbsp (30 ml) lemon juice

⅓ cup (80 ml) heavy cream

Garnish

Fresh black pepper

Parmesan cheese

Lemon zest

This is one of those side dishes that you just can't stop eating. It doesn't get much easier, or more satisfying, than this 20-minute pasta bursting with fresh flavors, featuring tender orzo pasta, lots of fresh spinach, marinated sun-dried tomatoes, vibrant lemon zest and Parmesan cheese. Enjoy as a side dish with my Salmon Piccata (page 52) or enjoy as a meatless main!

1. Press "Sauté." Add the butter and let it begin to melt. Add the shallot, season with salt and stir until fragrant, for 2 to 3 minutes. Add the garlic and chili flakes and stir for 30 seconds.

2. Add the lemon zest, the orzo and sun-dried tomatoes. Stir. Then, add the chicken broth and gently stir. Be sure to scrape all the orzo on the sides of the pot into the broth. Cancel the sauté mode.

3. Place the lid on. Press the "Pressure Cook" button until the display light is under "HIGH" and use the "-/+" button to adjust the time to 4 minutes. Be sure the valve on top is set to sealing. Once the orzo is done, quick release the steam.

4. Remove the lid once the pin has dropped. Add in the spinach, basil, Parmesan cheese, lemon juice and heavy cream. Stir well to combine.

5. Season with pepper and garnish with more Parmesan and lemon zest, if desired. Serve immediately.

TAWNIE'S TIPS:

- To make a chiffonade with the basil, simply stack the leaves, roll, and slice into thin ribbons.
- To reheat leftovers, heat a pan on the stove top over medium heat, add the orzo and pour in heavy cream until desired creaminess is reached.

RISOTTO PRIMAVERA

YIELD: 8 SERVINGS

TOTAL TIME: 40 MINUTES

For the veggies

1 large carrot, peeled and cut into coins

½ bunch asparagus, cut into 2-inch (5-cm) pieces

1 small zucchini, cut into half moons

1 small head broccoli, cut into small pieces

1 yellow squash, sliced into half moons

1–2 tbsp (15–30 ml) olive oil

1 tsp herbes de Provence

1 tsp kosher salt

¼ tsp black pepper

For the risotto

4 cups (960 ml) vegetable broth

1 tbsp (15 ml) olive oil

2 tbsp (28 g) unsalted butter

1 small yellow onion, diced

3 cloves garlic, minced

2 cups (394 g) Arborio rice, uncooked

¾ cup (180 ml) sauvignon blanc or dry chardonnay

This Risotto Primavera is what I like to call "comfort in a hurry." As you can see from the ingredient list, this risotto showcases plenty of veggies, fresh herbs and it's all tossed with bright lemon zest, salty Parmesan and butter! I'm swooning over the colorful vegetables and perfectly creamy risotto and it comes together with minimal effort. Risotto in the Instant Pot is easy to master and like my Tomato Basil Sausage Risotto (page 17), this is a relatively hands-off meal considering the traditional method!

1. Preheat the oven to 400°F (204°C). Line a baking sheet with foil and toss the chopped carrots, asparagus, zucchini, broccoli and yellow squash on the baking sheet with the olive oil and the herbes de Provence, salt and pepper. Roast for 15 minutes or until the veggies are tender and lightly browned. Remove from the oven and set aside.

2. To begin making the risotto, heat the vegetable broth in a medium saucepan over low heat. Keep the broth on low heat while you start the risotto. Add the olive oil and butter to the Instant Pot. Press "Sauté" and wait a minute or two for the Instant Pot to get hot. Add in the onion and sauté until fragrant and tender, for 3 to 4 minutes. Add in the garlic and stir for 30 seconds or until aromatic.

3. Pour in the Arborio rice and stir for 1 to 2 minutes to "toast" the rice. Deglaze the pot with the white wine and allow the wine to simmer for another 1 to 2 minutes. Pour in the warm vegetable broth.

4. Press "Cancel" to exit the sauté mode. Secure the lid on and press the "Pressure Cook" button until the display light is under "HIGH" and use the "-/+" button to adjust the time to 6 minutes. Be sure the valve on top is set to sealing. Once the timer sounds, quick release the pressure. Once the pin drops, remove the lid.

½ cup (70 g) frozen peas

½ cup (50 g) finely grated Parmesan cheese

⅓ cup (15 g) fresh basil, chopped

¼ cup (15 g) fresh flat leaf Italian parsley, chopped

1 tbsp (3 g) fresh oregano, chopped

1 tbsp (2 g) fresh thyme, chopped

Salt and pepper, to taste

2 tbsp (30 g) unsalted butter

2 tbsp (30 ml) lemon juice

1 tbsp (6 g) lemon zest

Garnish

¼ cup (34 g) toasted pine nuts

Finely grated Parmesan cheese

5. Stir the risotto well. Then add in the roasted vegetables, frozen peas, Parmesan cheese, all the herbs, butter, lemon juice and lemon zest. Taste and adjust the seasonings. Serve with toasted pine nuts on top and additional Parmesan cheese and enjoy!

TAWNIE'S TIP: Add in your favorite veggies based on what is in season! During the fall, I love this with roasted butternut squash and cauliflower. Don't you just love the fall?!

EASIEST CHICKEN WINGS WITH CREAMY PARMESAN DIPPING SAUCE

YIELD: 4-6 SERVINGS
TOTAL TIME: 30 MINUTES

1 cup (240 ml) water

2 lbs (908 g) chicken wings (party wings)

0.7 oz (19 g) dry Italian dressing seasoning mix

2 tbsp (30 ml) olive oil

1 tbsp (4 g) fresh flat leaf Italian parsley, chopped

1 tbsp (15 ml) lemon juice

Pinch of salt

Pinch of black pepper

Pinch of red pepper chili flakes

Dipping sauce

¾ cup (180 ml) mayonnaise

⅓ cup (80 ml) sour cream

½ cup (50 g) shredded Parmesan cheese

2 cloves garlic, minced

2 tbsp (30 ml) lemon juice

1 tsp apple cider vinegar

½ tsp Italian seasoning

¼ tsp kosher salt

This method for wings is nearly impossible to mess up! My husband is probably laughing right now because somehow, I always find a way to mess something up, but I promise this recipe never goes wrong! Cooking chicken wings in the Instant Pot allows them to get nice and tender and they are finished in the oven under the broiler so the skin can get nice and crispy. This method is sure to be your new favorite. Oh and that dipping sauce? SO GOOD. I'm not sure if I get more excited about the sauce or the wings but the combination is phenomenal!

1. Pour the water into the Instant Pot. Place the trivet or a steamer basket inside the pot. Toss the chicken wings in a bowl with the dry Italian dressing mix. Place them on the trivet steamer basket. Secure the lid and press the "Pressure Cook" button until the display light is under "HIGH" and use the "-/+" button to adjust the time to 10 minutes. Be sure the valve on top is set to sealing.

2. Combine the olive oil, parsley, lemon juice, salt, pepper and chili flakes in a small bowl. Once the timer sounds, let the pot sit undisturbed to allow the pressure to naturally release for 5 minutes. Then, quick release any of the remaining pressure. Once the pin drops, remove the lid.

3. Place the chicken wings in an even layer on a rimmed baking sheet lined with foil and a cooling rack on top. Spread the olive oil and herb mixture on top of the wings. Broil in the oven until the wings are nice and crispy, for 5 to 8 minutes—ovens may vary.

4. Meanwhile, whisk together all the ingredients for the dipping sauce. Serve chicken wings hot with the dipping sauce and enjoy!

TAWNIE'S TIP: Guess what?! If you have frozen wings, you can still make this recipe! Follow the same instructions but increase the cook time to 15 minutes. Easy-peasy.

BEEF SLIDERS WITH SUN-DRIED TOMATO AIOLI

YIELD: 8 SERVINGS

TOTAL TIME: 50 MINUTES

1 tbsp (15 ml) olive oil

1 yellow onion thinly sliced

1 cup (240 ml) beef broth

¾ cup (180 ml) cabernet sauvignon or red wine blend

2 lbs (908 g) boneless beef chuck roast, cut into 4-5 large pieces

2 tbsp (32 g) tomato paste

1 tsp kosher salt

1 tsp dried oregano

1 tsp Italian seasoning

1 tsp garlic powder

½ tsp black pepper

Sun-dried tomato aioli

1 cup (240 ml) mayonnaise

½ cup (27 g) sun-dried tomatoes, roughly chopped

4 cloves garlic, chopped

1 tbsp (15 ml) red wine vinegar or lemon juice

3 tbsp (45 ml) olive oil

⅛ tsp kosher salt

Pinch of red pepper chili flakes

For the sliders

Slider buns

Arugula

Cheese (I like pepper jack)

Any of your other favorite toppings

Tender, fall-apart beef piled high on a soft slider bun with melty cheese, peppery arugula and a generous slathering of creamy sun-dried tomato aioli. These are perfect for entertaining and always disappear fast!

1. Add the olive oil to the Instant Pot. Press "Sauté" and wait 1 to 2 minutes for the Instant Pot to get hot. Add in the onion and sauté until they are fragrant and tender, for 3 to 4 minutes. Press "Cancel" to exit the sauté mode. Pour in the beef broth and red wine. Nestle the beef into the pot.

2. Add the tomato paste, salt, oregano, Italian seasoning, garlic powder and pepper on top of the beef, but DO NOT STIR. Secure the lid on and press the "Pressure Cook" button until the display light is under "HIGH" and use the "-/+" button to adjust the time to 40 minutes. Be sure the valve on top is set to sealing.

3. Meanwhile, make the aioli by blitzing the mayonnaise, sun-dried tomatoes, garlic, red wine vinegar, olive oil, salt and chili flakes together in a food processor until they are smooth and creamy. Small bits of sun-dried tomatoes are OK.

4. Once the timer sounds, let the pot sit undisturbed to allow the pressure to naturally release for 10 minutes. Then, quick release any of the remaining pressure. Once the pin drops, remove the lid.

5. Shred the beef using two forks. It should be very tender and smell heavenly! Build your sliders with your favorite toppings and enjoy.

TAWNIE'S TIPS:

- This beef recipe is also uber delicious mixed in with Mom's Tomato Sauce (page 135) served over 20-Minute Parmesan Polenta (page 121).

- Optional, but I urge you to try it out: Brush the tops of the slider buns with melted butter, parsley and garlic powder. YUM!

ITALIAN WHITE BEAN DIP

YIELD: 8 SERVINGS
TOTAL TIME: 1 HOUR

For the beans

1 cup (180 g) dried white beans

4 cups (960 ml) water

½ tsp kosher salt

½ tsp garlic powder

½ tsp onion powder

For the dip

¼ cup (80 g) tahini

¼ cup (60 ml) mayonnaise

¼ cup (25 g) finely grated Parmesan cheese

3 cloves garlic, minced

½ lemon juiced

1 tsp kosher salt

1 tsp fresh oregano, chopped

1 tsp fresh basil, chopped

¼ cup (60 ml) olive oil, plus more as desired.

Garnish

Fresh basil

Parsley

Olive oil

This has turned into one of my family's favorite healthy snacks and it's just so easy to make. It's best served alongside vibrant, raw veggies, crunchy pita chips, crusty garlic bread or smothered on your favorite sandwich. Whatever way it's eaten is so delicious! My toddler eats it off the palm of her hands, so I think she has the right idea. Like her, you literally won't be able to keep your hands off (or out of) this yummy dip!

1. Add the white beans to the Instant Pot and pour the water, salt, garlic powder and onion powder on top. Stir and then place the lid on.

2. Press the "Beans/Chili" or "Beans/Grain" button, which should be set to 30 minutes on "HIGH" pressure. Be sure the valve on top is set to sealing. Once the beans are done, allow the pressure to naturally release for 20 minutes. Release any remaining pressure and then once the pin drops, remove the lid.

3. Drain the beans, but don't rinse them. Add the beans to the bowl of a food processor and add in the tahini, mayonnaise, Parmesan cheese, garlic, lemon juice, salt, oregano and basil. Process until the dip starts to come together and then slowly begin to stream in the olive oil and process until smooth. Taste and adjust the seasonings, adding more salt or olive oil as desired.

4. Garnish the dip with fresh basil, parsley and olive oil. Serve with crackers, garlic bread, or veggies.

TAWNIE'S TIP: If you have leftovers, simply bring the dip back to life by adding a generous drizzle of olive oil on top and garnish with some fresh herbs.

BABY PORTABELLA PEPPERONI PIZZAS

YIELD: 6 MUSHROOMS
TOTAL TIME: 15 MINUTES

6 (3-inch [7.5-cm]) baby portabella mushrooms

1.5 oz (45 g) pepperoni, diced

½ cup (56 g) shredded mozzarella

⅓ cup (75 g) marinara sauce

½ tsp Italian seasoning

1 cup (240 ml) water

These adorable mushrooms have all the flavors of pizza and are one of the easiest appetizers to make! Simply filled with cheese, pepperoni, marinara and a touch of Italian seasoning. These are easily customizable; just like you would add your own toppings to a regular pizza, feel free to add whatever you like in these mushrooms! Pop them under the broiler in the oven for 1 to 2 minutes so the cheese on top gets nice and bubbly and serve with plenty of additional cheese and marinara on top.

1. Wash and dry the mushrooms and discard the stems. In this order, stuff each mushroom with about 1 tablespoon of each the following: pepperoni, mozzarella, marinara and a pinch of Italian seasoning on top.

2. Pour the water into the Instant Pot. Line the steamer basket with foil, spray with nonstick spray and set in the pot. Place the mushrooms in the basket.

3. Secure the lid on and Press the "Pressure Cook" button until the display light is under "HIGH" and use the "-/+" button to adjust the time to 5 minutes. Be sure the valve on top is set to sealing. Once the mushrooms are done, quick release the pressure. When the pin drops, remove the lid. Carefully spoon out the mushrooms and serve with more cheese and marinara, if desired.

4. Optional step: Broil the mushrooms in the oven on a foil-lined baking sheet so the cheese gets golden and bubbly.

TAWNIE'S TIP: The baby portabella mushrooms I'm using are about 3 inches (7.5 cm) in diameter and perfectly fit in the Instant Pot (not the large portobello caps)!

20-MINUTE PARMESAN POLENTA

YIELD: 4 SERVINGS
TOTAL TIME: 20 MINUTES

4½ cups (1.1 L) chicken broth

1 cup (160 g) stone-ground polenta

½ tsp kosher salt, plus more to taste

Black pepper, freshly ground

4 tbsp (56 g) unsalted butter

½ cup (50 g) finely grated Parmesan cheese

1 tsp fresh thyme or rosemary

Creamy polenta is for those evenings when you're craving comfort food and this version is made without the fuss in less than 30 minutes. I have found the Instant Pot is the easiest, quickest and tastiest way to prepare it, and I know you'll be obsessed too! And as a mom, easy, quick and tasty are all high priority recipe must-haves! Serve as a side dish with my Beef Braciole (page 46) or with my Beef Ragu Pappardelle on top (page 38). With simple ingredients, this smooth and creamy polenta comes together quickly and everyone gathered around the table will devour this one!

1. Whisk the broth, polenta, salt and a few grinds of pepper together in the Instant Pot then select "Sauté."

2. Bring to a simmer for 2 to 3 minutes, whisking occasionally.

3. Press "Cancel" to exit the sauté mode. Secure the lid in place with the steam vent sealed. Press the "Pressure Cook" button until the display light is under "HIGH" and use the "-/+" button to adjust the time to 10 minutes.

4. Once the polenta is done, quick release the steam. When the pin drops, carefully remove the lid.

5. Add in the butter, Parmesan and thyme. Stir to combine. The polenta might look thin, but it will thicken as it sits. Taste and adjust the seasonings. I recommend adding in at least ½ teaspoon or more of salt and lots of freshly ground pepper. Serve immediately and enjoy! Store leftover polenta in the fridge for up to 2 to 3 days.

TAWNIE'S TIPS:

- Avoid using instant polenta. Any medium or coarse stone-ground polenta will work perfectly.
- Polenta thickens as it sits and tends to clump as it cools. To reheat, select the sauté mode and whisk in more broth or water to achieve a thin and smooth consistency again.

CROWD-PLEASING ARTICHOKE DIP

YIELD: 8 SERVINGS

TOTAL TIME: 20 MINUTES

½ cup (120 ml) chicken broth

1 (14-oz [400-g]) can artichokes, drained and quartered

4 cloves garlic, pressed

10 oz (284 g) frozen chopped spinach, drained

8 oz (232 g) cream cheese

½ cup (120 ml) plain Greek yogurt

½ cup (120 ml) sour cream

1 tsp Italian seasoning

¾ tsp onion powder

½ tsp salt

½ tsp red pepper chili flakes

2 cups (224 g) shredded mozzarella cheese

1 cup (100 g) finely shredded Parmesan cheese

Garnish

Basil

Pine nuts

For serving

Pita chips, bagel chips, etc.

This is the kind of dip you see people hover over at parties and they all beg to get the recipe. It's rich, creamy, plenty cheesy and filled with spinach and artichokes. You'll fall in love with this savory appetizer and adore the slight surprising tang from the sour cream. Overall, it's simply hard to resist. Like the name says . . . it's totally crowd-pleasing! I love it served on sliced baguette bread or pita chips.

1. Pour the chicken broth into the Instant Pot and add the artichokes, garlic and spinach. DO NOT STIR. Then, add the cream cheese, yogurt, sour cream, Italian seasoning, onion powder, salt and chili flakes. Once again, DO NOT STIR.

2. Place the lid on. Press the "Pressure Cook" button until the display light is under "HIGH" and use the "-/+" button to adjust the time to 4 minutes. Be sure the valve on top is set to sealing. Once the dip is done, quick release the steam.

3. When the pin drops, remove the lid. Give everything a good stir. It will look watery at first, but it's OK. It will thicken! Stir in the mozzarella cheese and the Parmesan cheese. Taste and adjust any seasonings as desired.

4. Transfer the dip to a bowl and garnish with fresh basil and pine nuts.

5. Serve with pita chips, vegetables, bread, crackers, etc. Enjoy!

TAWNIE'S TIPS:

- I hope this gets gobbled up on day 1, but if you do manage to have leftovers you can reheat the dip on the stove or in the microwave until it reaches the desired temperature.

- Be sure to add the ingredients in the order they are listed and do not stir them together. I'm so demanding, I know! But, this helps to avoid getting the dreaded "BURN" message on the Instant Pot.

ITALIAN STYLE WHOLE CAULIFLOWER

YIELD: 1 CAULIFLOWER HEAD
TOTAL TIME: 15 MIN

For the herb butter

4 tbsp (56 g) softened unsalted butter

1 tsp garlic, minced

1 tsp Italian seasoning

1 tsp kosher salt

½ tsp red pepper chili flakes

Freshly ground black pepper

For the caulifower

1 small to medium cauliflower head

1 cup (240 ml) filtered water

⅓ cup (33 g) finely grated Parmesan cheese

Garnish

Parmesan cheese

Fresh flat-leaf Italian parsley, chopped

I was blown away the first time I steamed an entire head of cauliflower in our Instant Pot! It turns out perfectly tender every time and it's ridiculously simple to make too. A whole cauliflower head smothered in a buttery garlic Italian seasoning spread. It's the perfect side dish to enjoy with my 20-Minute Creamy Chicken Marsala (page 41) or Whole Italian Chicken (page 55).

1. To make the herb butter, combine the softened butter, garlic, Italian seasoning, salt, chili flakes and freshly ground pepper in a small bowl.

2. Cut the leaves from the bottom of the cauliflower. Trim the stem of the cauliflower without cutting the florets so that the cauliflower can sit evenly on the trivet or steamer basket.

3. Spread the herb butter all over the cauliflower—I just use my hands for this part!

4. Place the trivet (or a steamer basket if you have one) down in the Instant Pot and pour 1 cup (240 ml) of water into the bottom.

5. Place the cauliflower head on the trivet or in the steamer basket. Secure the lid in place with the steam vent sealed. Choose the "STEAM" function and cook on high pressure for 3 minutes for crisp, tender florets or 4 minutes for a softer floret. Once the timer sounds, quick release the steam. When the pin drops, remove the lid.

6. Carefully remove the cauliflower and sprinkle with Parmesan cheese and fresh parsley on top. Serve warm and enjoy!

7. Optional step: To get a crispy crust on the outside of the cauliflower, place the cauliflower head in an oven-safe dish or on a baking sheet and broil for 2 to 3 minutes or until the cauliflower gets a nice crust.

TAWNIE'S TIP:

If your Instant Pot does not have the steam function, follow this guide:

- Smaller cauliflower heads: 3 to 4 minutes, "HIGH" pressure, quick release

- Larger cauliflower heads: 5 minutes, "HIGH" pressure, quick release.

BACON AND PARMESAN GREEN BEANS

YIELD: 4 TO 6 SERVINGS
TOTAL TIME: 30 MINUTES

1 lb (454 g) green beans

1 cup (240 ml) filtered water

2 tbsp (28 g) unsalted butter

2 tbsp (30 ml) olive oil

4 strips thick-cut bacon, diced small

2 tbsp (18 g) minced shallots

2 tsp (6 g) garlic, pressed

1 tsp Italian seasoning

1 tsp kosher salt

Black pepper, freshly ground

Garnish

Finely grated Parmesan cheese

Lemon zest

Black pepper

Bacon lovers, this one's for you. Here, vibrant green beans are steamed, while thick-cut bacon, shallots and garlic fill them with flavor. Green beans cooked in the Instant Pot hold their integrity and they're such a wonderful vegetable that absorbs whatever you mix with them. Everyone will flock to this side dish thanks to the healthful color of green beans cooked just until they are crisp-tender paired with salty, crispy bacon. With recipes as delightful and delicious as this one, serving green beans to the family is no feat.

1. Wash, trim and cut the green beans into 1-inch (2.5-cm) pieces.

2. Add the water to the bottom of the Instant pot. Place the steamer basket in and place the green beans in the steamer basket.

3. Choose the "STEAM" function for 0 minutes on "HIGH" pressure. Once the green beans are done, quick release the steam. When the pin drops, carefully remove the lid.

4. Remove the steamer basket with the green beans and drain the water. Place the pot back in and add in the butter and olive oil. Choose the "Sauté" function and once hot, add in the bacon. Cook, stirring occasionally, for 6 to 8 minutes. Once the bacon starts to get crispy, add the shallots and cook for 1 to 2 minutes. Then, add the garlic and stir for 30 seconds.

5. Add the steamed green beans in and stir to combine. Season with Italian seasoning, salt and pepper.

6. Remove from the Instant Pot and garnish with Parmesan cheese, lemon zest and black pepper.

TAWNIE'S TIPS:

- Partially freeze the bacon for 1 hour so it's easier to cut into small pieces.
- If your Instant Pot does not have the steam function, cook on high pressure for 0 minutes, or 1 minute for softer green beans.

"ROASTED" GARLIC SPREAD

YIELD: ¾ CUP
TOTAL TIME: 35 MINUTES

1 cup (240 ml) water
5–6 heads garlic
2 tbsp (30 ml) olive oil, divided
½ tsp kosher salt, plus more to taste

While it's true you cannot actually roast anything in the Instant Pot, you can still make a ridiculously scrumptious garlic spread in it and in half the time! The pressure cooker essentially steams the garlic and makes it perfectly creamy and soft, so it's easy to mash. I've found making my garlic spread with this method results in a more garlic-forward flavor which makes it ideal for adding into soups, serving as part of a charcuterie board, or stirring into pasta sauces. I even love adding in a bit of mayonnaise and making it into an aioli and using it with the Beef Sliders (page 114). Any way you use it, I know you'll love it!

1. Pour the water into the Instant Pot and set the trivet in the pot. Cut about ¼ inch (.75 cm) from the top of the cloves so you can expose the individual cloves of garlic.

2. Rub olive oil over the tops of the garlic. 1 tablespoon (15 ml) should be plenty. Place the garlic on the trivet and then put the lid on.

3. Press the "Pressure Cook" button until the display light is under "HIGH" and use the "-/+" button to adjust the time to 10 minutes. Be sure the valve on top is set to sealing. Once the garlic is done, allow the pressure to naturally release for 20 minutes. Release any remaining pressure and then remove the lid.

4. Carefully take out the garlic and let it cool for 15 minutes. Then squeeze the garlic heads into a small mixing bowl and discard the skins. Add in the remaining olive oil and salt. Mash and stir to combine. Taste and adjust salt as desired.

5. Use this spread in a variety of ways! Some of my favorite ways include spreading it on a crostini with fresh herbs, adding it into soups, rubbing it on chicken, adding it to a flatbread pizza, mixing it into homemade salad dressings, or using it for homemade garlic bread!

TAWNIE'S TIP: The awesome thing about this garlic spread? It lasts for up to a week in an airtight container in the refrigerator. I hope it disappears before then, though!

HOMEMADE RICOTTA

YIELD: 3 CUPS

TOTAL TIME: 2 HOURS 30 MINUTES

8 cups (1.9 L) whole milk

1 cup (240 ml) heavy cream

⅓ cup (80 ml) lemon juice, freshly squeezed

½ tsp kosher salt, plus more to taste

Garnish

Black pepper

Fresh herbs (rosemary, basil, thyme)

Olive oil

Once you make your own ricotta and realize how foolproof it actually is, you won't want to buy the store-bought stuff ever again. The texture and taste is superior to anything I've ever had out of the tubs from the store and as you can see from the ingredient list below, it doesn't require much! Just four simple ingredients to create the most luxurious ricotta and before you know it, you'll be slathering it on just about everything.

1. Pour the milk and heavy cream into the Instant Pot. Cover with a lid or a plate that fits your Instant Pot.

2. Press the "YOGURT" button and then press it again until the digital display reads "BOIL." Allow the Instant Pot to run its cycle. Once you hear a beep, this means it has completed and has reached 180°F (82°C).

3. Remove the lid. Remove the inner pot and place on a countertop trivet or a potholder. Pour in the lemon juice. Slowly and softly stir the lemon juice in and you will notice it start to coagulate. Stop stirring and allow it to rest for 10 minutes.

4. Line a fine-mesh sieve or colander with cheesecloth and place over a large bowl. Transfer the curdled milk mixture to the cheesecloth and allow the liquid from the cheese to drain at room temperature for 2 hours, or up to 4 hours for a firmer ricotta.

5. When the cheese is done draining, stir in the salt. Taste and add more salt as desired.

6. Serve the ricotta on your favorite pastas or as an appetizer on toasted crostinis with pepper, fresh herbs and olive oil.

TAWNIE'S TIPS:

- Store this dreamy ricotta in the fridge in an airtight container for 4 to 5 days.

- If you're extra like me, don't discard the leftover liquid AKA the whey. You can easily add it into smoothies, into soup stocks, use it to soak nuts or grains or use it for baking bread!

Staple Sauces

With so many wonderful Italian sauces to choose from, I narrowed down this chapter to my six favorite recipes. There is nothing quite like a pot of red sauce simmering on the stove, but when you're crunched for time and need some everyday staple sauces, these recipes will work wonders.

These sauces are all made with fresh, high-quality ingredients. Some are rich and hearty like my Mom's Tomato Sauce (page 135) and others are light but incredibly flavorful like our favorite Everyday Pesto (page 144).

My Everyday Pesto (page 144) is not made in the Instant Pot, but I just had to include a pesto recipe in this book! Plus, it's used in several recipes throughout this book, such as my Creamy Tomato White Bean Soup with Pesto (page 89) and my Pappardelle al Pesto (page 74). It's versatile and downright delicious and you'll find yourself quadrupling the batch. My recipe is a traditional basil pesto that uses pine nuts and basil and you'll want to spoon generous amounts over perfectly al dente, steaming spaghetti all summer long.

These sauces work beautifully with most pastas and heavy dustings of fresh Parmigiano to complete the dish. I especially love the Red Bell Pepper Sauce (page 139) not only with pasta but on pizzas or just for dunking a big hunk of crusty bread into. The same goes for the Quick Pomodoro Sauce (page 143)—use it in lasagna, stuffed shells, on flatbreads, etc. Also, make and use these red sauce recipes anywhere in this book where "marinara" is listed. Anytime fresh sauce can be used in place of jarred marinara, the meal is instantly elevated.

My staple sauces are quick to prepare, minimal, yet packed with flavor and complement all pastas. Hello, excellent comfort food!

MOM'S TOMATO SAUCE

YIELD: 12 CUPS

TOTAL TIME: 1 HOUR
15 MINUTES

2 tbsp (30 ml) olive oil, divided

1 large yellow onion, diced

1 red bell pepper, diced

1 yellow bell pepper, diced

4 cloves garlic, minced

½ cup (120 ml) cabernet sauvignon or red wine blend

1 cup (240 ml) beef broth

2 (28-oz [794-g]) cans crushed tomatoes

1 (28-oz [794-g]) can whole tomatoes with juices

1 tbsp (15 g) sugar

¼ cup (6 g) chopped fresh basil

¼ cup (15 g) chopped fresh flat leaf Italian parsley

1 tsp fresh chopped oregano

1 tsp kosher salt

½ tsp black pepper

½ tsp red pepper chili flakes

6 oz (170 g) tomato paste (optional)

My mom has a famous tomato sauce she traditionally makes and she lets it simmer for hours on end on the stove during the holiday season. I took her recipe and revised it just a tad to make it work in the Instant Pot and I couldn't be happier with the results. It's a classic, hearty, red wine–infused sauce that's perfect for pasta, dipping mozzarella sticks in, pizza, lasagna and more!

1. Add 1 tablespoon (15 ml) of olive oil to the Instant Pot. Press "Sauté" and wait a minute or two for the Instant Pot to get hot. Add in the onion and bell peppers. Sauté the veggies until they are fragrant and tender, for 4 to 5 minutes. Add in the minced garlic and sauté for 30 seconds.

2. Pour in the red wine to deglaze the bottom of the pot and allow the veggies to simmer in the wine for 1 to 2 minutes. Press "Cancel" to exit the sauté mode. Add in the beef broth, crushed tomatoes, whole tomatoes, remaining tablespoon of olive oil and sugar. DO NOT STIR.

3. Secure the lid with the vent in the sealing position. Press "Pressure Cook" until the display light is underneath "HIGH." Use the "-/+" button to adjust the time until the display reads 20 minutes. When the sauce is done, allow the pressure to naturally release for 15 minutes. Quick release any remaining pressure and when the pin drops, remove the lid.

4. Add in all the basil, parsley, oregano, salt, pepper and chili flakes. Use an immersion blender to blend the sauce until smooth. Taste and adjust the seasonings. If you'd like a thicker sauce, add in the tomato paste and simmer on the sauté "less" mode until the desired sauce consistency is reached, stirring frequently so the sauce doesn't burn or stick to the bottom. Alternatively, you can transfer to a pot on the stove to simmer to avoid burning the bottom.

5. Serve with your favorite pasta and enjoy!

TAWNIE'S TIP: This recipe makes a lot of sauce! You can freeze it if needed for up to 3 months. Allow the sauce to cool, divvy up the sauce into freezer safe containers (leaving room at the top for the sauce to expand) and that's it.

WEEKNIGHT BOLOGNESE SAUCE

YIELD: 8 SERVINGS

TOTAL TIME: 1 HOUR 10 MINUTES

2 tbsp (30 ml) olive oil

1 yellow onion, diced

2 large carrots, grated

3 ribs celery, diced

8 oz (226 g) mushrooms, grated

1 tsp kosher salt

¼ tsp black pepper

Pinch of chili flakes

Freshly grated nutmeg

2 bay leaves

3 cloves garlic, minced

2 tbsp (32 g) tomato paste

1 lb (454 g) ground beef

1 lb (454 g) ground pork

4 oz (114 g) pancetta

½ cup (120 ml) pinot grigio, sauvignon blanc or a dry chardonnay

1 (28-oz [794-g]) can crushed tomatoes

½ cup (120 ml) beef broth

¼ cup (60 ml) heavy cream

¼ cup (15 g) fresh flat leaf Italian parsley, chopped

Garnish

Parmesan cheese

Think cozy Bolognese, but let's make it fast and hands-off for weeknight comfort! This mouth-watering sauce recipe is the perfect addition to any lasagna or to toss with bouncy pappardelle pasta. It has a blend of ground beef, ground pork and pancetta, filled with veggies and a rich tomato-garlic base. You can't go wrong with this Italian classic!

1. Add the olive oil to the Instant Pot. Press "Sauté" and wait 1 to 2 minutes for the oil to get hot. Add in the onion, carrots, celery and mushrooms and sauté for 5 minutes. Season with salt, pepper, chili flakes, nutmeg, bay leaves, garlic and tomato paste. Stir to combine.

2. Add in the ground beef, ground pork and pancetta and cook, breaking up the meats with a wooden spoon until they are no longer pink.

3. Deglaze with white wine and cook 1 to 2 minutes.

4. Pour in the crushed tomatoes and beef broth and DO NOT STIR. Press "Cancel."

5. Secure the lid on and press the "Pressure Cook" button until the display light is under "HIGH" and use the "-/+" button to adjust the time to 20 minutes. Be sure the valve on top is set to sealing. Once the sauce is done, quick release the steam. Once the pin drops, remove the lid.

6. Stir in the heavy cream and parsley. Choose the sauté mode again and simmer the sauce for 10 minutes, stirring occasionally. Taste and adjust seasonings, as desired. Serve with your favorite pasta and garnish with Parmesan cheese.

TAWNIE'S TIP: Bolognese is meatier than it is saucy. So, if you're looking for a more saucy sauce, try my Quick Pomodoro Sauce on page 143, or Mom's Tomato Sauce on page 135.

RED BELL PEPPER SAUCE

YIELD: 4 CUPS

TOTAL TIME: 15 MINUTES

4 red bell peppers

1 (7.8-oz [230-ml]) jar fire-roasted red bell peppers; liquid drained

¾ cup (180 ml) water

½ cup (50 g) finely grated Parmesan cheese

¼ cup (6 g) chopped fresh basil

¼ cup (60 ml) heavy cream

2 tbsp (28 g) unsalted butter

2 cloves garlic, minced

1 tsp kosher salt

1 tsp Italian seasoning

1 tsp sugar

¼ tsp black pepper

This is a tomato-free sauce that utilizes both fresh red bell peppers and a jar of fire-roasted red bell peppers for a hint of heat. This sauce features a sweet bell pepper flavor and has the most gorgeous red-orange hue. It's enriched with lots of garlic and Parmesan cheese and the seasonings are minimal yet perfectly embody Italian flavors. It attains a creamy and fragrant texture even with a quick total cooking time—you'll be wanting to slurp this one up by the spoonful.

1. Wash the bell peppers and remove the seeds and membrane. Chop into large pieces and add them to the Instant Pot. Add the fire-roasted bell peppers and pour the water on top of the bell peppers.

2. Secure the lid with the vent in the sealing position. Press "Pressure Cook" until the display light is underneath "HIGH." Use the "-/+" button to adjust the time until the display reads 3 minutes. When the sauce is done, quick release the steam. Once the pin drops, remove the lid.

3. Switch to the sauté "less" mode. No need to drain the water. Add in the Parmesan cheese, basil, heavy cream, butter, garlic, salt, Italian seasoning, sugar and pepper. Then stir to combine. Using an immersion blender, blend until the sauce is smooth. Taste and adjust seasonings. Simmer on the sauté mode until desired sauce consistency is reached. It should be able to lightly coat a spoon. Be sure to stir frequently so the sauce doesn't burn or stick to the bottom. Alternatively, you can transfer to a pot on the stove to simmer.

4. Serve with your favorite pasta.

TAWNIE'S TIP: If you'd like a thicker sauce, like my husband usually requests, add in up to up to ¼ cup (66 g) tomato paste. Start with 1 tablespoon (15 g) and go from there.

CLASSIC BÉCHAMEL SAUCE (BESCIAMELLA)

YIELD: 2 CUPS

TOTAL TIME: 15 MINUTES

2 cups (480 ml) whole milk

4 tbsp (56 g) unsalted butter

4 tbsp (32 g) all-purpose flour

½ tsp kosher salt

⅛ tsp white pepper

⅛ tsp nutmeg, freshly grated to taste (optional)

This classic white sauce is silky, creamy, made with just a few ingredients and is really simple to make. Béchamel is great served over your favorite pasta, in a lasagna, spooned over baked salmon or with vegetables.

1. Microwave the milk in a glass measuring cup for 1 to 1½ minutes, or until slightly warm to the touch. Set aside.

2. Select "Sauté" less on the Instant Pot and melt the butter, moving it around the pot to melt evenly.

3. Add the flour and whisk to form a paste and continue whisking for 1 minute. Begin to add the milk in a slow, steady stream, whisking constantly.

4. The sauce will thicken and begin to gently bubble. Press "Cancel" to turn off the Instant Pot. The sauce is ready when it is thick enough to coat the back of a wooden spoon. Season with salt, white pepper and freshly grated nutmeg, if using. Taste and adjust seasonings as desired. Use the sauce right away with your favorite meal.

TAWNIE'S TIPS:

- Béchamel can be made and refrigerated for up to 3 days in advance. Reheat in a saucepan over low heat, adding milk if needed to loosen the sauce to your desired consistency.

- When seasoning, add 2 ounces (55 g) finely grated Parmesan cheese, Swiss or Gruyere to make this a Mornay cheese sauce.

QUICK POMODORO SAUCE

YIELD: 4 CUPS
TOTAL TIME: 30 MINUTES

1 tbsp (15 ml) olive oil

1 medium white onion, diced

2 cloves garlic, minced

Splash of water

2 lbs (907 g) fresh tomatoes, cut into quarters

1 large carrot, diced

6 oz (170 g) tomato paste

1 tbsp (15 g) sugar

2 tsp (12 g) kosher salt

1 tsp dried oregano

1 tsp dried basil

½ tsp black pepper

Garnish
Parmesan cheese

If you're looking for a fresh tomato sauce recipe, this is it. It's an economical and versatile red sauce with an irresistible flavor. After you sauté the onion and garlic, all you have to do is dump in the remaining ingredients and press start! It's light, fresh and just so delicious and easy. There are many versions of this sauce and I hope you love my take on it.

1. Add the olive oil to the Instant Pot. Press "Sauté" and wait 1 or 2 minutes for the oil to get hot. Add in the onion and sauté for 5 minutes or until soft and fragrant. Add in the garlic and stir for 30 seconds. Add a splash of water to the bottom of the pot, scraping any bits that may have stuck to the bottom. Press "Cancel" to exit the sauté mode.

2. Add the tomatoes, carrot, tomato paste, sugar, salt, oregano, basil and pepper and DO NOT STIR.

3. Secure the lid on and press the "Pressure Cook" button until the display light is under "HIGH" and use the "-/+" button to adjust the time to 15 minutes. Be sure the valve on top is set to sealing. Once the timer sounds, let the pot sit undisturbed to allow the pressure to naturally release for 10 minutes. Then, quick release any of the remaining pressure. Once the pin drops, remove the lid.

4. Use an immersion blender and blend until the sauce is smooth. Taste and adjust seasonings, as desired. Serve with your favorite pasta and garnish with Parmesan cheese.

TAWNIE'S TIP: Almost any kind of tomatoes will work, but I love using San Marzano or Roma.

EVERYDAY PESTO

YIELD: 1 CUP
TOTAL TIME: 10 MINUTES

2 cloves garlic

½ tsp kosher salt

1 oz (28 g) fresh basil leaves

⅓ cup (48 g) pine nuts

⅓ cup (33 g) freshly grated Parmesan cheese

⅓ cup (80 ml) extra virgin olive oil

2 tbsp (30 ml) lemon juice

Salt and black pepper, to taste

I just want to eat this pesto with a spoon. It's *that* good! This vibrant, creamy, basil-forward pesto is simple to make and a great way to add a pop of color to any meal. You'll see this recipe used in this book on my Creamy Tomato White Bean Soup with Pesto (page 89) and it is of course a fabulous addition to any pasta (page 74 for Pappardelle al Pesto). But of course, it can be used in countless ways: omelets, pizzas, bruschetta or sandwiches. Be sure to use a mild, mellow olive oil so it doesn't distract from the fresh basil.

1. Using a mortar and pestle, crush the garlic and salt for about 1 minute. Then, begin to add in the basil leaves, in 2 to 3 additions, crushing until a paste forms, for 5 minutes. Be sure to blend the ingredients in a circular motion, as opposed to a vigorous up-and-down motion.

2. Add in the pine nuts and crush them in. Then, add in the Parmesan cheese, in increments, until combined. Slowly drizzle in the olive oil, about 1 tablespoon (15 ml) at a time, and stir with a spoon until emulsified.

3. Lastly, add in the lemon juice and season to taste with salt and pepper. Use tossed into your favorite pasta, topped on pizza, coated on roasted veggies, dolloped on an omelet, etc.

TAWNIE'S TIPS:

- Use a food processor if you don't have a mortar and pestle. (I just love the mortar and pestle for the most basil-forward flavor.) Add all the ingredients except the olive oil to the food processor and pulse until coarsely chopped. Then, slowly start to stream in the olive oil until the pesto is emulsified.

- Freeze leftover pesto by scooping pesto into ice cube trays and freeze until solid. Top the pesto with a little bit of olive oil to prevent browning. Once frozen solid, pop out of ice cube trays and store in a baggie in the freezer until ready to use.

ACKNOWLEDGMENTS

First and foremost, I want to thank you. A cookbook of course is nothing without the people buying the book and making the recipes. You are the reason I wrote this. Thank you for giving me that reason, that opportunity and the chance to share these recipes with you. It is my hope these recipes will inspire you, bring you together around the table with loved ones and nourish you. I'll never be able to explain in words how much it means. Thank you, thank you, thank you!

I want to thank my husband, Cameron. He has fully supported me from the early days of me figuring out my path to now and over the years has continued to motivate me to do what I love. Thank you for being there for me through all the emotional days filled with tears and for putting up with me in general (I can be a lot). You whole-heartedly make me a better person and I am so grateful to call my best friend my better half.

Thank you to my Momma, Yvonne. I owe so much of my success in life to you. You were a tremendous help with watching Arya while I worked. You made countless grocery store runs for me. You proofread and edited my work for the book and were always happy to be a taste tester. I am so lucky to have a close relationship with you, mom, and now being a mother myself, I deeply appreciate our relationship even more. We have a good laugh now over my firstborn being a girl. It's karma since I was a lot to handle growing up!

Thank you to my Daddy-o who is not with us anymore. I miss you; I love you and you gave me the courage to pursue anything difficult in life.

To my family, Teagan, Meghan, Tommy, Kayden, Ryan, Karen, Ana, Nancy, Scott and Grammie. Thank you for your endless support and listening to me rant on about this book for so long. You all have helped in so many ways, whether it was watching my daughter or simply critiquing and tasting a recipe—all your help never went unnoticed and I am thankful for each and every one of you.

Thank you to all my readers and followers on Kroll's Korner. Like I mentioned earlier, you are all my reason why. I am forever grateful to have such an amazing online community and group of people to inspire me—so thank you for being there both in the online space and for supporting this book.

Last but not least, thank you Page Street Publishing for the opportunity to write this book. You have been wonderful to work with, so thank you for letting me share my passion with the world!

ABOUT THE AUTHOR

Tawnie Graham is a registered dietitian nutritionist who lives in Fresno, California, with her husband, Cameron, daughter, Arya, and their two dogs, Bella (Aussie) and Rugby (Yellow Lab). She is the owner of the popular food blog, Kroll's Korner, where she shares realistic, easy-to-make meals just like the ones you see in this book. She is a food photographer, videographer, recipe developer, mom, wife, lover of wine and cookies, blogger by day and professional dishwasher by night. Tawnie believes in making cooking fun and reasonable so you can nourish your body with simple and flavorful recipes. And yes, even as a dietitian, you can find Tawnie eating plenty of pasta and not just kale salads!

INDEX